"AS OUR HEADS ARE BOWED ..."

NOEL DAVIDSON

AMBASSADOR

BELFAST ◆ **GREENVILLE**
NORTHERN IRELAND   SOUTH CAROLINA

"AS OUR HEADS ARE BOWED ..."
Copyright © Ian R. K. Paisley
and Noel Davidson

First published September 1998

ISBN 1 84030 030 2

Ambassador Publications
a division of
Ambassador Productions Ltd.
Providence House
16 Hillview Avenue,
Belfast, BT5 6JR
Northern Ireland

Emerald House
1 Chick Springs Road, Suite 203
Greenville,
South Carolina 29609, USA
www.emeraldhouse.com

CONTENTS

FOREWORD 5

MY CALL TO PREACH 7

SOME PERSONAL RECOLLECTIONS 21

INTRODUCTION 33

1. A WHOLE NEW WAY OF WALKING 37

2. MR. RICO'S CIRCUS 46

3. RISE UP AND GO 50

4. THE UNPARDONABLE SIN? 58

5. THE HIDE-AND-SEEK BIBLE 61

6. RIGHTFUL RECOGNITION 73

7. AN URGENT MESSAGE 77

8. CHAIN SMOKER 86

9. DO IT YOURSELF! 89

10. IMPERSONATION! 100

11. HEAVEN'S BARRICADES ON HELL'S BROAD ROAD 104

12. NOT A POLITICAL MATTER 113

13. A CUPFUL OF SIN 118

14. TELL YOUR CHILDREN...AND YOUR CHILDREN'S CHILDREN 131

15. PEGGY AND TED 138

16. A LITTLE CHILD SHALL LEAD THEM 145
17. THREE BOOKLETS FOR TWO BOB 150
18. IT'S GOOD TO TALK 160
19. A SOLEMN WARNING 163
20. WELL, THAT'S IT! 170
21. THIS MARRIAGE NEEDS A MIRACLE 174
22. HAPPY WITH THE HOLD-UP 188
23. A DIFFERENT SET OF GOALPOSTS 191
24. STAND BACK AND WATCH
GOD AT WORK 208
25. LITTLE LOST SHEEP 212

FOREWORD

BY DR. IAN R. K. PAISLEY, MP, MEP

❖

Dear Reader,

In my early days as a preacher my revered father, a great book man, introduced me to Spencer's Recollections.

Later I obtained a copy of Spencers further volume on the same subject. These books recorded conversions and incidents in the life of a preacher and soul winner. They inspired me with a desire to have trophies to lay at the feet of my blessed Lord who had saved me and called me to be a preacher of the gospel and a winner of souls.

He who tastes of the soul-winner's wine will not want to partake of any other beverage. The winner of souls has meat to eat that no one who has not partaken of the same, can in any way appreciate. Lord, evermore give me this meat!

I remember the first soul, a dear mother, who came to saving faith through my preaching in the Leighmore Faith Mission Hall, Ballymena. How I rejoiced over that soul and watched her progress on the pilgrimage to heaven. Lasting fruit is the true accrediting testimony of a pure gospel ministry.

This book records a few of the vast number of people who have been transformed by the free grace of God, under my preaching.

E'er since by faith I saw the stream
Thy flowing wounds supply,
Redeeming blood has been my theme
And shall be till I die.

To God's great Name be all the glory.
Oh, that my Saviour were your Saviour too!

Yours in Christ,

From the happiest preacher in the world,

You R. K. Paisley

Eph 6:19+20

Ian R. K. Paisley
September, 1998

MY CALL TO PREACH
IAN R. K. PAISLEY

❖

**TO BE A PREACHER OF THE GOSPEL OF OUR LORD
JESUS CHRIST IS THE GREATEST OF ALL CALLINGS. IT IS
THE HIGHEST HONOUR WHICH GOD EVER COMMITTED
TO ANY MORTAL.**

Angels - the highest of all God's creatures, for man was made a
little lower than the angels - were not given this honour. They are in
fact ministers to the ministers of God's gospel of His Son, servants
of the servants of the Word of God.

The preacher is divinely chosen and divinely commissioned. No
amount of money paid to a theological faculty or to ministeral
college professors can make a man a preacher. True preachers are
divinely made, not humanly manufactured. Modern ecclesiastical
jargon talks of a minister being called to a particular congregation.

New Testament preachers are sent, not called. *"How shall they
preach except they be sent"* Romans 10: 15. The call of the people
does not make a true gospel preacher. He must be sent of God.

Every real gospel preacher magnifies his office. He trumpets
with the apostle Paul. Galatians 1: 15-16: "But when it pleased God,
who separated me from my mother's womb, and called me by His
grace, to reveal His Son in me that I might preach Him among the
heathen; immediately I conferred not with flesh and blood."

I Timothy 1: 12: "And I thank Christ Jesus our Lord, Who hath
enabled me, for that He counted me faithful, putting me into the
ministry."

About my own sending into the ministry, I neither thought it nor sought it.

After finishing schooling in Ballymena Technical High School I determined to make my future in agriculture.

The Paisleys were of farming stock and I aimed to enter Greenmount Agricultural College and although I spent most Saturdays on the farm of Mr. Charles Beattie of Dunfane, who was a great help to me both spirutally and agriculturally, I required to spend some time in full time farming.

Where better to go than the place of my family roots, Sixmilecross, County Tyrone. Mr. and Mrs George Watson and their son Harold opened their home on the hill, down the road from Sixmilecross towards Carrickmore, to me.

There I was initiated into all the jobs of farming, from feeding hens to milking cows, from ploughing to threshing, from potato dropping to potato gathering, and from rearing calves to rearing pigs.

Now, the Sixmilecross Evangelistic Hall had fallen on evil days. George Watson determined to keep the door open. The only service in the week was an afternoon Sunday service which was attended by the Watson family, the Bob Kyle family, an elderly lady from the village, and sometimes George's neice, Miss Lena Hastings, joined them.

George asked me to preach one Sunday and very reluctantly I consented.

The congregation consisted of Mr. & Mrs. Watson, their son, Harold, Mr. Bob Kyle and his two sons and the elderly lady already mentioned. Consequently another lady insisted she had been present. She must have been dreaming!

I decided to preach on the man going down from Jerusalem to Jericho (Luke 10: 30-37) who fell amongst thieves.

The Sunday afternoon arrived and I was confident I had enough thoughts to keep me going for a good twenty to twenty-five minutes. However, I was a man who also fell amongst thieves. My thoughts were all stolen from me when I stood up to speak and I managed about two minutes. Being forced to flee from my text I fled in desperation to the next text. I did two minutes on that text on the house of Martha (Luke 10: 38-42) and sat down in total confusion - total time four minutes.

I vowed secretly that preaching was not for me and that I would stick to the plough and not the pulpit.

Coming out, Mr. Bob Kyle, a distant cousin of mine, said, "Ian, if you spoke for four minutes when you are sixteen, at seventy you'll preach for hours!" Bob did not realise that he was a prophet and neither did his friends!

A short time afterwards I was introduced to the art and backache of turf cutting. They called it turf cutting but the cutting is just the first stage of the process. There is no better place to meditate than in the bogland, turning over the turf to the rays of the sun. I left the farmhouse early and rode a bicycle as far up the mountain as I could and then had to walk up the last steep pathway. The happy thought always comforted me that it would be free wheeling all the way down. When I arrived I worked all day turning the turf and setting up those dried in threes or fours.

I thought long and hard and decided to try preaching again.

The appointed Sunday came once more. The congregation, the same to my recollection, but this time I got what the preacher knows as 'liberty'. I got through quite comfortably. Bob Kyle advised me to go back to the bog- land.

Then other opportunities came and the time arrived when I had to face up to the will of God for my lfe. I surrendered to God's will but was anxious to know what it was to be.

One day when harrowing corn in 'Frank's land' (a small holding called after its original owner) I had to stop, because the Lord Jesus, with that still small voice only known to His people, was directing me. His orders were for me to plough in another sphere. To sow a different seed and expect a different harvest. That sphere was gospel preaching, that seed was the gospel seed, that harvest was the harvest of precious souls.

I was not disobedient, and my revered father, to whom from a human standpoint, under God I owe my ministry, arranged for me to enter the Barry School of Evangelism which is now the Theological Seminary of Wales. I entered in the fall of 1942, during the war, aged 16 years.

That School was sourced from the 1904 Welsh Revival. One of the great preachers of that Revival, Rev. R. B. Jones, was its founder.

On his decease his son, who was tainted with modernistic falsehoods against which his father had so firmly battled seized the school. The Rev. B. S. Fidler, the main tutor, and others pulled out and saved the school for Biblical truth. Mr. Fidler became its Principal.

Two very important things happened there in relation to my preaching.

I developed doubts as to my call. I knew I must be sure beyond doubt. If there was any nagging doubt that the happening in 'Frank's land' was not as definite as I thought, then I must know.

The only confidence that a preacher can have to nerve him in the darkest days is the total assurance that he has the Divine Call and that God has pledged Himself to be with him.

In the school we rose each morning at 6 am except on Saturdays and Sundays. One morning after dressng I knelt down determined to get this grave matter settled. There must be no more doubts. If still in doubt I would leave and return home.

As I was praying, these words lit up my heart. They came like the flash of a search light, 'Follow me and I will make you fishers of men'.

I rose relieved and happy, but it was short-lived. The devil was not going to give up so easily. The satanic suggestion was, 'You thought of that verse because you wanted to. It was an auto-suggestion.'

I went downstairs to breakfast at 8 am, having listened to the devil. My doubt was as large as ever. Then I prayed, "O God, confirm this word to my heart if it be so for me."

After breakfast the Principal always read the daily portion of the Geneva Bible School, Switzerland, a sister school to our own. The scripture portions were only issued in the French language and Mr. Fiddler was the only person in United Kingdom who used them.

What was the portion? It was the portion in Matthew 4: 19 which contained the words, 'Follow me and I will make you fishers of men.' A great Hallelujah arose in my breast. 'It's only a coincidence,' whispered the devil.

My faith was stronger however, and I looked for yet another token for good. Yes, and I got it.

At nine o'clock we had our opening devotions in the Lecture Hall. We used hymns from the Geneva Bible School hymnal which Mr. Fidler had translated from the French. Our school was the only place in the UK which had these hymns in English.

The following hymn was the one which Mr. Fidler choose to open our devotions:

Boats and nets they left behind them
Those disciples by the lake,
Christ to follow; He would teach them
Men alive henceforth to take.

We must follow this same Master,
If we also souls would win;
Faithfully proclaim the Gospel,
Snatching men from dens of sin.

By Thy grace, then loving Saviour,
Leaning on Thy strength alone,
To Thy call to follow fully,
Thee as Lord I gladly own.

May I follow without murmur,
Serve Thee with a heart of praise,
Love Thee without ever faltering,
Thee obey throughout my days.

Self-denying, my cross taking;
This, O Lord I've made my choice;
Thee, and Thee alone to follow,
I have heard Thy loving voice.

Thou hast called me, Who art faithful,
O my blessed Lord and God;
Give me grace that I may follow
In the path that Thou hast trod.

My soul shouted with joy and I sang with great gusto. The doubt fled away forever. I was called to be a preacher of the Word of God and I never doubted it again.

The second important thing which happened was my schooling in learning to preach.

I met a unusual Christian brother when I was at the Barry School - Teddy Sherwood.

Teddy was a former welterweight champion boxer of the South of England and he had a huge gold belt to prove it.

In his unconverted days he had been a hard living, hard drinking, hard gambling, hard speaking, out and out child of the devil.

Grace fought a battle with him and the champion was defeated. He became the captive of grace, a child of God and a devout follower of the Lord Jesus. He was ablaze with a desire to tell others of what the Lord Jesus had done for him. So anywhere and everywhere in the open air he would start preaching.

He was a unique sinner, now he was a unique sinner saved by grace.

He came with his great gold belt in his hand. Through the last hole in the belt he inserted a long piece of string which he plaited. Wherever there were people he would use his belt as a whip and to what effect! People gathered to behold the sight, a gold belt shining in its perfection and the cracking of the whip at its end. He did this until the curious crowd was large.

Then he stopped, laid the belt along the ground, took off his coat, rolled up his sleeves, loosened his tie and approached the crowd.

He would accost one of them and present one of his cauliflower ears and request the person to pinch it. He then showed the scars on his back and chest. "This," he cried, "is what the devil did for me." Then he would say, "Oh, if only I could roll down my skin from my ribs and show you my heart. It's whiter than snow through the precious blood of my Saviour."

Then he started to preach, dancing with the same actions of the boxing ring. "I'm fighting the devil," he would explain.

Now, Teddy had a very loud voice but he had never learnt to use it properly. He spoke from his throat and not from his diaphram and after ten minutes his voice always broke.

If he only had learned the lesson of the speaker's rhyme:

Start low
Go slow
Don't blow
Rise higher
Catch fire

he would have done so much better.

Now, when his voice left him Teddy needed another preacher until he got what he called his 'second wind'. He required a gap filler.

I was Teddy's gap filler. He gathered the crowd, he preached, he broke down, he called me in and when his second wind came he ordered me out and the pattern was repeated three or four times.

This is how I cut my preaching teeth. I was a lackey in the Ted Sherwood school of preaching.

I learned to run the gauntlet of the crowds. I had to be able to answer and never show any resentment when Teddy summarily dismissed me by a wave of his hand or as quickly ordered me back again as he panted for his returning wind. I learned the preacher's rhyme and benefitted from it. One thing was sure, Teddy never let me blow.

One Sunday afternoon, I remember so well, Teddy decided to have an open air service amidst a carnival in the centre of Barry Island.

During the war years on Sunday afternoons vast multitudes of servicemen and women gathered there for jollification, pleasures and sin. It was Vanity Fair with a vengeance. Teddy loved the place, for there he got his loudest but also his largest crowd.

The service started in its usual way. Teddy and his belt were the preliminaries. Then came Teddy's challenge to the devil and his castigation of his former master. Then came the preaching as Teddy gave the devil his due.

If ever I prayed as the crowd heckled, jeered and scorned and laughed, I did then.

I dreaded what would happen when the gap filler had to intervene.

Sure enough it came. Teddy started to gasp, his voice gave way and his command was hoarsely given, "Get in there and keep it going!"

Imagine to yourself the large hostile crowd, the star performance given and a tall, thin, beardless, seventeen year old stripling taking over.

I started low but I did not get time to do anything else but to go slow. I had a rude and what became an impertinent heckler. She was a young woman in the grey-blue of the WAAF - The Women's Auxiliary Air Force.

She screamed, "Young man (she might have better said young boy) how do you know there is a Jesus Christ?"

In those days I was ignorant of women. I thought you could talk a woman down (I have learned better since) so I went on preaching. She got real angry. She came into the ring. The crowd took up her chant. She came right up to me shouting. "How do you know there is a Jesus Christ?"

What do you do in such circumstances? There is only one escape route - the path of prayer. I cried in my heart, "Oh God give me the answer. You've got me into this, now get me out!"

Like a flash the answer came. I stopped. I addressed the young woman somewhat like this.

"Why do you ask a question when you yourself know the answer?"

She shouted, "I don't know the answer. You don't know it either!" and the crowd showed its teeth.

I said, "You do know the answer and you yourself will tell this crowd. I have but three questions to ask you and your answer to the third one will be the answer which you say you do not know."

The crowd by this time was quiet and eager to hear my questions.

I said, "What day is it?"

She replied, "Sunday."

I said, "What month is it?"

14

"June," she snapped.

"What year is it?" I asked

She saw the trap. The crowd howled turning their jeers on her. She hesitated, and then said "1943."

"Ah," I said, "where did you get that year from?"

She ran back in confusion into the crowd.

I said, "1943 AD - in the year of Our Lord Jesus Christ. Every time you look at the calendar or your diary you have proof there is a Jesus Christ. The great question is, 'What will you do with Him?'"

By this time Teddy had received his wind and the gap filler's job was done for a little while.

That incident had two sequels.

The first happened a few days afterwards.

Some of the young woman's companions in the WAAF sought us out and told us that she had been greatly disturbed. They asked us to visit her in her billet. Teddy and I with others did so. She would not come out but held a conversation with us through the window. She was troubled in soul and was hardening her heart. Only eternity will reveal the outcome. I left her sorrowfully.

The gospel is a savour of death unto death!

The dying thief rejoiced to see
That fountain in his day,
And there have I, though vile as he
Washed all my sins away.

The other thief refused to see
That fountain in his day,
And there may you as vile as he,
Throw your last chance away.

The second sequel came to my knowledge during 1997 when, as Moderator of the Free Presbyterian Church, I opened our first church building in Burryport, Wales.

I travelled down from London in a police car accompanied by my protection officers, and I requested them to go via Barry Island.

When we arrived there I went to the spot of that Lord's Day service and related the above story to them. We then motored on to the opening of the church.

At the beginning of the sermon I told the story of the Barry Island incident to them..

At the end of the service a gentleman approached the pulpit.

He said how interested he was to have heard me report the Barry Island incident. Then he amazed me by affirming, "I was there."

He said he was in the Navy. His ship had just arrived in Barry Docks and it was his first day ashore for many, many weeks. He decided to enjoy himself to the full so he headed for the carnival.

He was confronted with Teddy's crowd, then he saw the preacher give up and a tall young boy take his place. He moved nearer. Then he saw the WAAF, enjoyed the banter but was suddenly and strangely arrested by my answer.

It was an arrow fastened in a sure place. He affirmed that for fourteen long years it haunted him, sometimes more powerfully than ever before and sometimes just in the back of his mind. However, at the end of fourteen years he got gloriously saved.

When he saw the announcement he decided that it was his bounden duty to travel a very long way to encourage the preacher to continue to preach Christ and Him crucified.

You can rest assured we had a Hallelujah time.

The gospel is the savour of life unto life.

And so, that is how I preached my first sermon and cut my preaching teeth.

PAUL'S WORDS TO A YOUTHFUL TIMOTHY - "LET NO MAN DESPISE THY YOUTH," (I TIMOTHY 4: 12)

Mr. Fidler suffered from a severe ulcer which at times left him a prey to awful sickness. He was a man of many talents. He could speak fourteen languages and could preach fluently in about seven. Although himself an Englishman he preached eloquently in the language of the land of his adoption, Wales.

Nearly every Lord's Day he was away preaching and in the war years he was in great demand at special services in the largest of churches. As a preacher of the old school he was called in to help with those who still loved the old ways and the old truths. You can read more of these men in the book "The Champions".

Most of the older students were busily engaged in pulpit work on the Lord's Day. The youngest with little experience had more Lord's Days free from preaching. I attended the Princess Street mission where an up and coming preacher named Ivor Powell was earning his spurs.

One Lord's Day Mr. Fidler had a bout of his ulcer sickness. That night he was to preach in one of the largest churches in one of the valleys some ten miles away. He thought that by afternoon he would be better and with his dogged determination he would be able to fulfil this important agreement.

By early afternoon he grew worse and he sent for me to come to see him. He said, "I cannot possibly make it. Now, as there is no one else here I have no other option but to send you in my place." I paled and felt as sick as the man giving me the order!

It meant a bicycle ride of over ten miles. It meant addressing a large congregation in an influential church and I had no sermon to hand. However, there was no way out so I was soon on my way.

I decided I would speak on the rich fool examining his thoughts, his soul and his end. Today I probably would have alliterated it as 1. His Deliberation, 2. His Determination and 3. His Damnation. As I cycled I meditated and prayed.

I entered the valley with time to spare and when I came to the village everybody seemed to be heading up the hill around and upon which the village was built. I thought foolishly that there must be a football match or something about to take place in the sports arena, hence the crowds!

At the top of the hill the people were entering a large Chapel, as the Welsh Protestant Dissenters places of worship were called.

I read the notice board and to my horror it was the church where I was to be the substitute for Mr. Fidler. I was scared but there was no turning back.

I wheeled my bicycle round to the back of the church and entered into a room at the rear of the pulpit. It was the room where the deacons met before taking their seats of pre-eminence in the front of the church. These special great seats were situated below and around the pulpit.

A middle aged man was there and I explained Mr. Fidler's illness. He cried out, "Has he arranged a substitute?" I said, "Yes" and he replied, "That's good." Then he asked, "Who is the substitute? Has the substitute arrived?" I replied, "I am the substitute." I thought he was going to faint. He said, "No, you are far too young to fill the pulpit here." Inquiring my age and hearing I was only sixteen years old he said with great authority, "No, you cannot preach here!"

I was relieved. I said, "I'll stay for the service." He hesitated and said, "No, you wait here I'm going to call the deacons."

The pillars of the church assembled. The door closed and these sturdy Welsh miners were going to decide my fate. I felt like a murderer waiting for the black-caped judge to send me out to be hung by the neck until I was dead!

Their deliberations over, these sober-faced men called me in. They said that because of the circumstances, the large crowd assembled in the church (no doubt because of Mr. Fidler's standing) that there was nothing else to do but to let me preach. They said if Mr. Fidler saw fit to pick me as his substitute they had faith that I must have at least some qualification.

The leading deacon gave me the Order of Service and the hymn numbers and opened the door into the Chapel. I saw a large church with a circular gallery well filled. There were many hundreds but to me it seemed more like thousands.

I worked through the Order of Service. The singing was up to the highest standards of the Welsh singing talents and my spirit was helped.

Then I opened the Book, read the passage about the rich fool and launched into the gospel message. I got unusual liberty. God's Spirit gave the lad with the gospel loaves a special anointing and the congregation responded. The Welsh call it the 'howel'.

At the after meeting, (which always followed each service since the 1904 revival days) the senior elder told the congregation the background of my coming, gave me the highest eulogy of catching the howel and said that he believed some day the world would hear of me. I was very humbled for I had learned that it was not by might, nor by power, but by My Spirit saith the Lord.

One of the congregation took me to his home, gave me a sumptuous meal and sent me away rejoicing. The rejoicing was short-lived. Riding over a railway crossing I ripped my rear tyre and had a puncture. I wheeled the bicycle back to the home where I had been treated so kindly. I had some difficulty in finding it but eventually did and the kind brother made the necessary repair. He was a friend indeed. I'm sure in the reward day he will not be passed over.

I again set out but a great rain storm broke out and I was soon drenched to the skin.

Calamity followed and I had another flat tyre. It was black out for the war of the Hun bombers was at hand at their murder work. I saw a glimmer of light and approached the door of a house by the roadside. The door opened. I explained to a strange looking man who answered, my plight. He didn't let me finish. He ordered me away with language that made my blood curdle.

So there was only way back and that was to walk. It was about four miles. At last with the water running out of me, dog tired, wearied and ready to collapse, sometime in the small hours, I made the College. Mr. Fidler had stayed awake to here how I did. He had been praying and his prayers had been answered.

I got dried out, took a mug of hot cocoa and fell into bed. It seemed about five minutes and I was being rudely pulled out of bed. The duty of the student who sounded the handbell to awaken the others was to await for a response. If it did not come it was his duty to get the sleepy head out of bed.

Dennis Parry, afterwards martyred for Christ in the Congo, was carrying out his duty as bell boy. He didn't know the circumstances of my coming back the night before.

I, however was enraged, with righteous or unrighteous indignation, I know not. I seized him unceremoniously, pushed him out of my room and through the door across the landing into the water tank room. I nearly baptised him again by the deepest immersion.

I slammed my bedroom door and slept the hour until seven o'clock. Then I arose and joined the others in the lecture hall.

Dennis looked at me sheepishly. I explained what had happened, apologised profusely for my indefensible behaviour, asked his forgiveness but mildly warned him in the future he should not jump to quickly to conclusions when I did not rise immediately at 6 o'clock. Like the real saint he was, Dennis was magnanimous and our friendship was forged even closer.

My wife and I erected a memorial to the martyrdom of my friend from College days and his wife and two children, in our Church, Martyrs Memorial. They have received the highest accolade in God's gift - the Martyrs Crown.

The noble army of martyrs praise Thee O God!

His memorial in the Church reads:-

Dennis Parry
Missionary & Martyr

Youngest of a family of six.
Mother died in boyhood.
Converted when twenty years old.
Led to prepare for missionary work through Keswick Convention in 1937.
Imprisoned in Cardiff for refusing to allow the war to stop his college preparation for the mission field.
Fellow student with Dr. Paisley at what is now the South Wales Bible College.
Went to Congo under the Unevangelised Fields Mission.
Great passion for souls.
Wife, Nora, a missionary nurse.
Last mission post, Bodela.
Martyred with wife and two children, Andrew and Grace by the Simba rebels.
Survived by two older children Hazel and Stephen.
"Faithful unto death".

SOME PERSONAL RECOLLECTIONS

❖

THE WORST SINNER ON THE RAVENHILL ROAD

Samuel Chadwick once told one of his students, 'Raise a Lazarus in your sphere of Christian service and the people will come to see him and you, the preacher that saw him made alive by your gospel preaching'.

'Who is the worst sinner on the Ravenhill Road?' I asked my church elders, 'because I want to see him saved!' They looked at me in unbelief, then they named a man, the old drunk of the Road. He started to booze when he was twelve years old, now he was almost seventy and still at his cups. Every night he was thrown out of the local pub and could be seen staggering his way along the road and through an entry to his house in the area known as the Lagan Village, near my church.

I prayed for that man. He came to church and sat on one of the forms (no posh pews in that church in those early days), on the right side of the pulpit. I filled my gospel gun every Sunday night, got him in the sights and fired both barrels at once, but my target never as much as blinked! At the end of each sermon he complimented me! One night I preached a rip-roaring sermon on booze, and gave 'Boss Alcohol' a real hammering. At the church door, and smelling of whiskey, he exclaimed,'An awful evil, this booze!' But I didn't let up.

One day his daughter sent for me. She said, 'The old man is ill. He has taken to his bed and he wants to see you.' I hurried round to her home where he was now staying. All the houses in that street had half-moons - the woman of the house would scrub the front door-step every morning and also a half-moon in front of it on the pavement, so all the houses had a scrubbed half-moon outside their front doors. I stepped over the half-moon and knocked on the door - there were very few door-bells on the red-brick terrace houses in those days. The old man's daughter opened the door and showed me in to the 'good room' as the front room with its window looking onto the street, was called. The room had been made into a bedroom for the convenience of the old man, and on the bed, almost completely covered by the bedclothes, lay my stubborn hearer. I sat down on a chair beside the bed. He whispered, 'Close the door I don't want her (referring to his daughter) to hear'. I obeyed, then said, 'Pull down the bedclothes from your face, I want to see you'. He obliged. Our conversation went something like this:

'I'm sorry you are sick'.

'I'm not sick'.

'Then why are you in bed?'

'I'm suffering with the burden of my sin,' he groaned.

'Hallelujah!" I shouted. 'I'm glad about that. You need a real dose of conviction of sin. You have wilfully rejected Christ over and over again. You are a guilty, lost, ill-deserving, undeserving and hell-deserving sinner.'

'I know it!' he cried.

'I hope God will soak you in conviction. Remember, if you are going to be saved you must have no hope or no trust in anything or anybody else except the Lord Jesus and Him alone.'

'Are you not going to do anything for me?' he sobbed.

'No, I cannot do anything for you'.

'Oh!' he sighed, 'I thought you could. What will I do?'

'Christ alone must save you, you must come to Him and throw yourself upon Him and Him alone." I told him.

'I'll come!' he cried.

We engaged in prayer. The young preacher of the Ravenhill Road and the worst sinner on the Road knelt together at the Cross, and the worst sinner was saved by amazing grace alone. His drinking companions gave him until the week-end but that week-end saw him saved and sober, the first week-end for almost fifty-eight years. They then gave him until the 12th July, Orangman's Day, but he was still saved and sober. They further gave him until the 12th August, Londonderry Day, but he survived, that as well. Then they said, 'He'll never get past Christmas Day,' but he did. They then mocked and said, 'The old man has got a life-sentence'. His reaction to this was 'The new man has got everlasting life'.

When he was called Home to Glory what a funeral we had! Crowds came and they who had witnessed his transformation. He preached his best sermon in his death. We promised, before he died, next time we would meet one another at the Golden Gate. In the Father's House the preacher and the worst sinner on the Road will praise God for ever for saving sinners like us.

All these once were sinners,
Despised in His sight,
Now arrayed in pure garments
In praise they unite.
Unto Him who has loved us,
And washed us from sin,
Unto Him be the glory
For ever, Amen.

THE WIFE-BEATER

Moore Street, at the foot of the Ravenhill Road, with its many homes and families, was the target of my evangelistic drive.

I became acquainted with every family and sought to bring to them the gospel of the Blessed Saviour.

There was one house - hovel would be a better description - to which I could not gain entry. In it dwelt an evil man who was known to be a vile beater of his wife. One night the neighbours heard the cries of his wife as he beat her - a beating from which she never really recovered. It was widely believed in the neighbourhood that the beating, if it did not actually kill her, certainly accelerated her death. Of course there was no real evidence, and moreover, no-one in the street wanted the man's aroused enmity targeted on them.

If I knocked on that door once, I knocked dozens of times. One day after knocking I heard a sound. The man was there! I kept knocking vigorously and eventually I knew that at last I had got my man. I also knew that when he saw me he would slam the door in my face, so I determined that once he opened the door I would shove it wide open and rush on into the room at the back. This is exactly what I did. I heard the front door slam and he came down the hallway, boiling with rage. When he saw me sitting on a box which served as a chair he angrily demanded to know the meaning of my behaviour. I told him I had a message from his best friend. The dialogue went something like this: 'I have no friends, and certainly not a best one', he snarled. 'That's where you are wrong. This friend loved you so much that he died for you.' 'Come off it', he shouted. 'No, I'm speaking the truth, and I must impress upon you the honesty of my errand'.

Little by little I got the gospel across. My earnestness seemed to dent his defences a little. I then knelt down and prayed before leaving . I called a few times after that and he always opened the door promptly. I kept the gospel arrows flying to his mind, conscience and heart.

One day he broke down and told me of his evil ways. He confessed his appalling brutality to his wife, the mother of his son. Anguish overcame him. I brought to him the gospel balm, the sweet healing of the Saviour's blood, and beside the old wooden box two hell-deserving sinners knelt down, one a sinner saved by grace and the other a sinner lost in sin, but when we rose, it was two sinners saved by grace.

Some years afterwards I attended a meeting in Whiteabbey Free Presbyterian Church where Sammy Spence and the Coalmen's Testimony Band were conducting a special service. In the first row of the Band I noticed a beaming figure, and something told me I knew him. I searched my memory and then I knew who it was - the man from Moore Street. After the meeting I accosted him along these lines: 'You weren't selling coal when I first met you.' He smiled broadly as he replied,'No, but you remember the day when Jesus washed all my sins away.'

Happy day, happy day,
When Jesus washed my sins away.
Hetaught me how to watch and pray,
And live rejoicing every day.
Happy day, happy day,
When Jesus washed my sins away.

HOW JOE BLACK BECAME JOE WHITE

Joe Black was a lost soul in time and in his folly planned to become a lost soul in eternity.

He had stood bail for a friend who was in deep trouble and as a fool he was skipped bail. Joe was left literally cleaned out of all his money.

The shock was too much for him. Bitterly disappointed with his friend and more bitterly disillusioned with his own life he decided to booze up and throw himself into the Lagan at the Ravenhill Embankment.

He carried out the first resolve but God in His great mercy prevented the second from happening.

My young people from the church conducted an open air service every Saturday night at the gates of the Ormeau Park on the Ravenhill Embankment.

I was with them when Joe Black, helplessly intoxicated, came staggering along to go to a watery grave and a lost sinners hell.

I was ever on the trail for souls at these open air meetings and saw the drunk man pull himself hand over hand along the park railings. I caught up with him. Our conversation went something like this:

I said, "Man, I have news for you, God loves you."

"If you knew who I was you wouldn't even talk to me. But I intend to drown myself tonight."

"It doesn't matter what I feel, but it does matter what God says and feels," and I quoted a gospel text.

In spite of his alcoholic stupor that text lit a fuse in his memory. He had been brought up to attend gospel meetings in his home town and the scripture was not unknown to him.

I said, "Let's go down to the Church at Shamrock Street and we'll pray together."

He blurted out, "I couldn't make it, I'm drunk."

I said, "I'll carry you!"

With Joe half on and half off my back I got him to the meeting house. I was always counted a fool so I was glad to live up to what they said about me!

Afterwards, I asked Joe, "What happened then?"

He replied something like this.

"You carried me to the church through the back door and down to the little room at the front. You laid me down on the form and you left me, closing the door behind you.

I sat there dazed. Then suddenly I heard a very loud voice. It was not the voice of preaching, it was the voice of praying. It was you talking to your God.

I was sobered up in a moment by what you were praying. You said something along these lines.

'Lord, you have promised to save to the uttermost. This man is a poor, drunken wretch, a potential suicide. I ask you to save him. He must be saved so that I can boast of your faithfulness. If you don't save him I'll have to quit the ministry. I could stay on if this prayer was answered.'

I was sobered and a cold sweat broke upon me. I would be responsible of driving this man out of his church. I must not do such a thing.

I had scarcely resolved that when you re-entered the room. Very simply and solemnly you explained the way of salvation and challenged me to quit my evil ways and come to Christ. I wept and said, 'I will, I will, I will.' We got down on our knees and with your arm around me you led me to the Saviour. The sunshine of heaven burst upon my soul, my burden disappeared in an instant and I looked on my Blessed Saviour and He looked on me and we were one for ever."

That was a Saturday night. The next night Joe Black, now Joe White, was in the Sunday evening gospel service. He waited behind. He said, "Preacher, I want to ask something. Last night I was drunk and I stank of booze but in the room we knelt together and I really met Jesus. I'm sober now, there's no smell of drink on me and there'll never be again, with God's help, but I want to go back into that room and kneel down and do it again. Christ got drunk Joe Black last night. I want Him to get sober Joe Black tonight."

We went into the room, shut the door and we were shut into heaven as sober Joe cried to the Saviour Who had saved him when he was drunk to take him now he was sober.

Formal orthodoxy might criticise this but orthodoxy cannot function without evangelistic unction.

When Friday came I worried about Joe. Every Friday of his working life he had gone from the Shipyard to the pub. He had never taken his wife home a full pay packet. I prayed. What I needed was not so much prayer as faith. I needed it then and I need it today so that the devil of unbelief might be cast out.

On Sunday Joe was in church. I could hardly wait until the service ended so I could hear how he fared on Friday night.

I said to him, "What about Friday night Joe?"

With a twinkle in his eye he said, "I did what I always did. I made for the pub. Oh but don't be alarmed. I went and stood in its doorway. I took of my old duncher (cap) and I thanked God that never again would I be going into the pub. I screwed my cap up and I said, 'Thank you Blessed Lord for saving Joe Black.' I put my hand into my pocket and said, 'For the first time my wife will get a full pay packet. God save her and my son as well.'

And God answered Joe's prayer far more abundantly than Joe could either ask or think.

O Ravenhill by the Lagan
Thou still to me art dear
And if one soul from that district
Meets me at God's right hand
My heaven, will be two heavens, in Emmanuel's Land.

THE CHURCHMAN

I was having a holiday break in Bangor when I received an urgent message from a young Christian lady who attended our services that her uncle was seriously ill in the Royal Victoria Hospital in Belfast. He had been diagnosed with terminal cancer.

He was a strong churchman, an office bearer in the Church of Ireland. Shattered by the news he discovered that his churchianity brought him no inward peace or no rest for his soul. He urged his niece to seek me out and request me to visit with him.

I left Bangor immediately and made my way to the RVH. He welcomed me and with great haste and concern told me his story.

It went somewhat like this.

"I was brought up in the Church of Ireland and attended Sunday school. I learned the Church Catechism. 'Who gave thee this name? My godfathers and godmothers in my baptism wherein I became a child of God, a member of Christ and an inheritor of the Kingdom of Heaven.' And I believed it.

When I grew older at my Confirmation the Bishop laid his hands on my head and told me I had received the Holy Spirit. And I believed him.

I took office in the Church and became a member of the Select Vestry and served as a church warden. I believe it was well with me as I was a constant communicant at the sacrament of the Lord's Supper.

Then I was diagnosed with cancer and I started to search my heart and soul. All my churchianity became as nothing. It was a mere performance. I had no peace, no assurance and I was terrified not so much with death but what came after it.

I am pinning my hopes on you. I believe you can help me."

I realised I had to be very blunt and very honest. This man was depending on fleshly religion and my powers were as useless in the matter of his soul's salvation as any other minister's.

I said most earnestly. "I cannot help you. I am no better than your own clergy in the matter."

"What?" he exclaimed, "and I thought you could do something for me."

"No," I said, "but I know Someone who can!" He sat up in the bed. "Tell me," he said, "Who is that?"

I said, "The Lord Jesus Christ. It's not the church you need, it's not baptism you need. Baptism cannot save. Of course it has an important place in the New Testament but not in the salvation of the soul. As far as you is concerned it can make you wetter but no better.

Partaking of communion cannot save you. You must be saved first before you can truly partake of the Supper of our Lord. Unredeemed you only add to your sin when you take communion. You eat and drink damnation to your own soul, as the Scriptures state."

"Then how can I truly and really come to Christ?" he asked.

"You must come as you are, confessing you are a lost sinner, and putting your faith in Christ alone for salvation.

Just as I am without one plea,
But that Thy blood was shed for me,
And that thou bidst me come to Thee,
O Lamb of God I come, I come."

Jettisoning all his trust in churchianity and protestant religiosity he came simply, in prayer, to the One who says, "Him that cometh unto Me I will in no wise cast out." John 6: 37 and, "Whosoever shall call on the Name of the Lord shall be saved." Romans 10: 18.

His cancer went into remission for a while. He was taken from the Royal to the City Hospital . He witnessed with radiant face and the happiness of that happy day experience when Jesus washed all his sins away. He once had religion, now he had Christ Himself.

I was with him the day he died. He was weak but radiant.

I quoted the great Shepherd's Psalm to him.

"The Lord is my shepherd," and he repeated it sentence after sentence after me.

When we came to the verse, "Yea though I walk through the valley of the shadow of death" he asked to be propped up in bed.

We raised him up and rearranged his pillows and he repeated the lines.

Then we came to the words, "I will fear no evil." Sitting up, he said, "I will fear ..." he stopped and shouted out, "NO, NO, NO evil." Three times he cried out "No". The whole ward heard him.

Then we quietly finished the Psalm. In a short space of time he had gone to the Father's house. He dwells, as the Psalm says, "in the house of the Lord FOREVER."

THE BUSINESSMAN WHO MADE IT IN THE NICK OF TIME

He was a well made, smallish man. He was of the bull dog breed and a real 'goer'.

His business was in top gear. He translated his own 'go' into his business and so it was successful.

But he was mad. His wife, his son and his daughter got saved under my preaching. That really angered him. When I passed his shop door he came out, stared at me in wrath and then went in and slammed the glass door of his business. I prayed the cut-glass would break but it was a prayer not in the will of God for it was never answered.

Along with his wife and family I prayed God would save him. That prayer was in the will for God for it was answered.

One day, out of the blue, I got a message from his wife that he was seriously ill in the Clark Clinic of the Royal Victoria Hospital.

I had no car at the time and I asked a friend to take me there.

It was late evening when we arrived and the main door of the Clinic was locked. I rang the bell but there was no response. My driver said, "Come back in the morning." I replied, "If that man sent for me he must be in a dangerous state. Tomorrow will be too late!"

I went around to the back of the hospital and found an open window. I got my driver to give me a leg up. As I reached the floor of the hospital kitchen a nurse ran in and demanded to know what I was up to.

I mentioned the man's name whom I had come to see and she said, "He's been crying for you all day. You're just in time."

She tore up the stairs, and I went after her. She led me into a private ward. The man was in an oxygen tent. He threw it back and cried, "Thank God you've come. Lead me to Christ."

There with the oxygen tent covers thrown back I had the joy of seeing his wife's prayers answered, his daughter's prayers, his son's prayers answered and the church's prayers answered.

He was easy to lead. The Spirit was there and the Saviour received him and heaven touched earth once again as a sinner came home to the Great Lover of his soul.

The sharp businessman only made it in the nick of time. Not long afterwards he was in eternity.

That story had a sequel.

At his funeral service in the home I told the thronged congregation, inside and outside, of his conversion. Three of his closest friends were there. They were broken and wept. Afterwards as they spoke with me one of them said, "It will surprise you to know that a sinner like me when I heard my companion was so ill, prayed that some way you would get to the hospital and lead him to Jesus."

The three of them professed faith in Jesus Christ as the result.

"Where sin abounded grace did much more abound."

I want to record my deep gratitude to Noel Davidson for patiently and diligently listening to these stories of grace and then visiting many of the persons involved and obtaining first hand accounts. He narrates them all superbly. He had the patience of Job in getting appointments with me!
To my daughter Cherith for setting the type and designing the layout of the book and to my darling wife Eileen, ever my unfailing help meet, for proof reading the same.

- Ian Paisley

INTRODUCTION

❖

S aul was an arrogant, rebellious, religious activist when God stopped him in his tracks one day. Dramatically. Abruptly. In the middle of the road. And in the resulting encounter, Saul had his name, his nature, his whole life's work, and his eternal destiny all changed. For good.

Paul, once Saul, loved to tell people about how it happened, too. He did it often. To great crowds and powerful people his message was always the same. God had saved him, and made 'a new man' of him. On that road that day.

And when he told that story it usually made an impression. Caused a stir. One way or another.

People, down the centuries, have always loved to hear a gripping testimony to God's saving grace, and still do so today. They find it fascinating.

People love to read, or hear, of other people's experiences.

So, when first approached by the publishers, to compile a book of testimonies of people who had been saved under the ministry of

Dr. Paisley, over more that fifty years, I was very pleased. But I also had a problem.

I was pleased to be given the opportunity to research these stories, focussing upon someone whom God has used so mightily, but my problem was, "How many testimonies do we want in this book?" There must be hundreds, I reckoned.

The answer to my question about how many, was, "Twelve. We will aim at twelve full testimonies. Twelve is a good Scriptural number." (Something to do with the tribes of Israel, the apostles, and the gates of the new Jerusalem...).

I was happy enough with that. It was a reasonable target.

However, when I began to work on the project, interviewing a tremendous variety of people, I soon realized that the testimonies fell neatly into two distinct categories. There were the real live stories, told to me by living subjects, the converts themselves. And there was the indispensable assortment of anecdotes recounted to me by Dr. Paisley and his wife, Eileen.

When I began to sift through the wealth of material at my disposal, I realized that there would have to be many more than twelve testimonies in the book, to do the subject any sort of justice. So I decided to divide the stories into their two natural sections.

The longer chapters in this volume, the odd-numbered ones, are the testimonies related to me by the subjects themselves (except 'The Hide-and-Seek Bible' where Jack Davidson's widow, Clara, very graciously helped me out). The even-numbered chapters are the shorter stories, recounted to me by Dr. Paisley, his wife, and others.

This book, entitled 'As Our Heads Are Bowed...', from the opening words of many impassioned appeals, "As our heads are bowed, and our eyes are closed, and the people of God are praying...", covers an amazing range of stories. These testimonies represent, in a very small way, the extent to which Dr. Paisley has been used of God to see literally thousands of souls saved, across the continents of the world. To complete it I have had many conversations with people who were saved in Northern Ireland, telephone calls to England and Canada, and an eyewitness account from Rev. David Mc Ilveen who accompanied Dr. Paisley to Africa!

INTRODUCTION

The incidents in this book involve a wide cross section of people. And places. Subjects range from a footballer to a fish merchant, from the family to their housekeeper, in venues as varied as auction rooms and living rooms, enquiry rooms and advice centres. Even a circus tent!

These are by no means all the stories that could be told of men, women and children who have been led to faith in Christ through Dr. Paisley's preaching. They are only the tip of the iceberg.

However, I have had to make a selection from those suggested to me, and I trust that you will find this book a blessing.

If you are one of the very many who have been saved through Dr. Paisley's ministry, and your story is not included, or if you know of someone who goes to your church, and 'she or he has a great story', please bear with me. I didn't know about you. Or them.

Meantime, enjoy the book. And if you enjoy it, buy one for a friend.

Our desire is that through this collection of testimonies, some person, or people, will come to know the Saviour. If that happens, Dr Paisley and his wife, Eileen, will be delighted. So, too, will all the subjects, who have so willingly co-operated with me in the compilation of this collection.

And above all there will 'be joy in the presence of the angels in heaven'.

The Bible tells me so.

Pray that it may be so.

NOEL I. DAVIDSON
September 1998

1

A WHOLE NEW WAY
OF WALKING

❖

The Second World War brought about many changes in the life style of the people of the city of Belfast. And for those with children, it brought about the most dramatic change of all. A move to the country for safety. A flit. Evacuation. However, for the Douglas family this was no strange thing. They belonged to the country.

When John Douglas was born, his father and mother lived not far from Newtownards, Co. Down. If some of the sounds his childhood ears picked up had influenced him, John would have followed a totally different lifestyle. He would have grown older with a passion for speed. His home stood at the roadside. There, on the other side of a small garden, the world-famous drivers in the Tourist Trophy Race sent their cars roaring and dipping as they zoomed along, scorching past his door at an awesome, breathtaking rate! But he was born to participate in another and better race, with a more enduring prize in view.

During the war years, the little family went to stay on Grand-father's farm, a couple of miles from Ballygowan. His parents were anxious that their family should attend Sunday School every Sunday, and so John, his sister and two brothers, walked to Ballygowan Presbyterian Church Sunday School. They had no option but to walk. There was no public transport. Especially on Sundays. But they didn't mind. They saw the beauty of the countryside throughout the changing seasons. And at Sunday School they learnt the Catechism, and great chunks of the Bible off by heart.

After the War, in 1945, the Douglas family moved back to live in East Belfast. So they had to change church. And Sunday School. They started to attend Megain Presbyterian Church on the Newtownards Road. This church was quite a distance from where they lived, and the family who had never complained about long walks in the country, began to moan about long treks through city streets.

Some friends were going to a Sunday School in a small church on the Ravenhill Road. It was called Ravenhill Evangelical Mission Church.

The family soon started to go there on a Sunday afternoon with their friends. It was so much more convenient.

John and his brothers and sister liked that Sunday School. There they had dedicated teachers who wanted to see their young pupils brought to know the Saviour. And they taught them, simply, the way of salvation. John had a lady teacher sometimes. He thought she was just great. She seemed to have such a genuine interest in him.

As the children became more accustomed to the church they started to attend the Sunday evening services as well. And it was there they first met the new minister. A tall lean man called Ian Paisley. Mr. Paisley was ordained minister of the church in 1946. And young John liked to hear him preaching. He was so fiery. So sincere. So much in earnest. He preached to get the message across. It really seemed important to him.

The more often he heard the Gospel proclaimed, the more completely the young lad became convinced that he should become a Christian. Come to Christ as Saviour. But he wasn't sure just how you came. It all seemed far too simple to him. Come and be saved.

Believe and live. There must be something in there that he hadn't heard about yet. Something much more complicated.

So he kept putting it off.

'Anyway, I am far too young to make an important decision like that', he told himself.

'Why do you need to bother about this salvation business when all your mates at school seem to get along fine without it?' he asked himself, many a time.

'You better be prepared,' he warned himself, totally falsely as it was to turn out, 'if you become a Christian you will never be able to enjoy yourself again.'

In spite of all the excuses, however, he could never seem to banish the thoughts of the importance of this whole matter from his mind.

One Sunday afternoon in September, 1946, John decided that he could put it off no more.

He wanted to come to Christ.

He needed to come to Christ.

He would come to Christ.

As the other children filed out of Sunday School, John remained behind. Intentionally. He meant business.

All the Sunday School teachers were moving into a small back room for a meeting, when one of the men became aware that he was still there. Alone. The moment of decision had come.

The concerned yet determined boy had no hesitation whatsoever in telling this friendly man what was on his mind. "I would like to be saved", he said.

The teacher was delighted, but posssibly not feeling confident enough to deal with a seeking soul himself, or perhaps deciding that there was someone else much better qualified to deal with such matters, he replied, in a happy fluster, "Wait there and I will bring the minister".

In a few moments time the new minister emerged from the little room at the back, and came over to speak to John.

Sitting down beside the young lad he opened up his Bible, and after reading from it in a number of places, he explained , very clearly, the way of salvation. He told John about sin, and how that everybody in the world was reckoned to be guilty before God. He spoke of the death of Christ and that how He, by that death on Calvary had provided an atonement for that sin. All that John, or indeed anybody else had to do was to come to Him. Believe in Him. Accept Him by faith.

Then he read the promise contained in John 6 v 37. "...Him that cometh to me I will in no wise cast out."

When he had finished reading and explaining, Rev. Paisley suggested that they should kneel side-by-side at the seat, while he prayed.

As the minister prayed for him that day, John Douglas came, with child-like faith, to the Saviour, realizing, and accepting that Jesus had died to take away his sin.

As they rose from their knees, John's young heart was filled with an indescribable joy. He knew that something powerful, something wonderful, had taken place in his life. He knew immediately that he was a child of God. The son of a King.

When John told Rev. Paisley of his faith in Christ, the new minister gave the lad wise counsel as to how to live as a Christian. "It is important that you read your Bible and pray every day", he advised. "For in the Bible God speaks to you. And through prayer you have the opportunity to speak to God. To praise and thank Him for all that He has done for you, and to bring before Him the needs of others, and your own burdens and concerns".

All that sounded reasonable enough to the new convert. He would certainly look forward to it. Then Rev. Paisley touched on something with which John just secretly reckoned that he might have a bit more of a problem though.

"And don't be afraid to tell others about your faith in Christ", the kindly big man continued. "Romans ten and nine tells us to confess with our mouth the Lord Jesus, as well as believing about Him in our heart. It's all part of it. It will give you a real sense of joy to tell others that you have got saved."

Young John tried to hedge his answer to that one. He didn't really see the need to tell anybody about what he had just done. It was a purely personal matter, he told himself. This, however, was really only an excuse because he didn't know how he would go about telling anybody. How would he begin to 'confess with his mouth the Lord Jesus'? What would he say? People would just laugh at him, he was sure. Think he had turned into some sort of a religious nut.

When at last he stepped out into the advancing chill of an autumn late-afternoon, he discovered that nearly everyone else had dispersed. So he walked home alone, his mind and emotions awhirl. He felt joy and peace in his heart. But yet the tranquility was tinged with trepidation.

He determined on that amble homeward that he would tell his parents about his commitment to Christ, first. It would be easier to tell them than anybody else. He knew they loved him dearly. And wouldn't hurt him for anything. But what would they say when he told them?

As soon as he arrived home, John told his parents what had happened. Told them that he had come to Jesus. Had become a Christian.

To John's relief, and slight surprise, they treated this news, which was so important, so vital to him, in a very matter-of-fact let's-wait and-see kind of manner. They reckoned if it kept John happy, and it didn't involve them having to fork out any money, it was probably an O.K. sort of thing. Time would tell.

Days, then months, passed. Young John was so happy in the Lord. He hardly ever missed a meeting in the Ravenhill Evangelical Mission Church. And he didn't go alone either. His two brothers, David and Robert, were always with him. And in a short time they also became Christians as well.

All three of these babes in Christ loved their new young minister. They never missed an opportunity to hear him speak. Hung on every word.

He was very tall this Rev. Paisley. And he walked then with a sort of a stoop, shoulders held forward. The whole of his upper body seemed to move in one rigid piece. It was quite a distinctive gait.

So John and his brothers started to walk like that. In all serious-ness. Stooped slightly forward, body stiff, arms swinging. Well, wasn't that how you had to walk when you were saved?! They were learning fast these young chaps! And they didn't even know at that time that Paul had once written to the Corinthian believers and told them to be followers, or imitators, of him, as he in turn was an imitator of Christ! (1 Cor. 11 v.1)

As he grew into teenage and as he continued to grow in faith and in his love for, and zeal to serve, his Saviour, John began to take part in the Christian Endeavour at the Church. This proved to be an immense help. Then he became a member of the Church, and became even more involved in the whole range of its activities. Praying in the prayer meetings, teaching in the Sunday School, speaking to Christians, and preaching the Gospel, both in his home church, and elsewhere, all provided opportunities for the keen young worker to cultivate his talents in the Lord's service.

Then he met Bob Scott, who had been converted one Sunday night at Ravenhill. Though once a wild "blue" man, a Linfield Football Club supporter from the other end of town, he was now completely changed.

Bob was older than John, but he recognized in the younger man, an ability that could be effectively channelled into Christian service. Bob soon made a name for himself as one powerfully gifted in prayer and open-air work. He suggested that they commence an open-air witness together.

When they told Rev. Paisley about their burden in relation to the commencement of a regular open-air witness, his reaction was typically brief and brusque. Yet it was both sensible and spiritual.

"We will get together and pray about it first", he told them. And they did.

Those prayer meetings became a turning point in the lives of the three men involved, and, later, affected many more.

John Douglas resolved to serve God with his whole heart. And for the whole of his life. Ian Paisley prayed for guidance in his life. For blessing. For revival. Bob Scott also entered into full-time Christian work.

An overwhelming sense of the power and presence of God was evident in those prayer times. As soon as all three of them had prayed once they each started all over again to open up their hearts to God. Such was the sense of urgency. Of conviction. Of God's love for lost souls.

Rev. Ian Paisley continued to preach, earnestly, fervently, every Sunday. And every other time during the week when given the opportunity. The hand of God came upon him and he preached in the fulness of the Spirit.

The prayer for revival that had begun with three believers praying about an open-air witness, developed into a regular weekly special prayer time. This in turn led to the commencement of all-night prayer meetings, when a group of earnest men met and cried to God for blessing. For the salvation of souls. For revival.

God answered those sincere requests in a mighty way.

Many people came to faith in Christ.

It became a regular thing for at least one person to be saved at every Sunday evening service. It was expected. Disappointment led to deep heart-searching on the rare occasion when a Sunday went past without a real movement of God being experienced.

In 1951 the Free Presbyterian Church was established. With John Douglas as one of its founder members.

With his overriding interest in outreach work John soon became convinced that he should enter full-time Christian ministry. So he began training. In a brand-new set-up.

A Theological Hall was opened at the new Ravenhill Free Presbyterian Church. The lecturers were Rev. Ian Paisley, Mr. Paisley's father, Rev. James Kyle Paisley and Dr. H.H. Aitcheson. Three of the first students to enrol were Cecil Menary, John Wylie, and a young man called John Douglas. They were all keen to be useful for God. To see souls brought to the Saviour.

When he had completed his studies, John launched himself enthusiastically into Christian work. Asssisting in campaigns conducted by Rev. Ian Paisley. Serving as counsellor at various missions.

A season of spiritual blessing during a Gospel outreach in Ballyhalbert Orange Hall led to the formation of a Free Presbyterian Church in Portavogie, in 1956. The first permanent minister there, in that pioneering work, was Rev. John Douglas. This was a new experience for John. The sole charge of his own congregation.

As the Free Presbyterian Church developed apace during the 1960's, new congregations began to spring up all over Northern Ireland.

Having been in Portavogie from 1959 until 1966, Rev. Douglas was then asked to employ his recently-acquired church-establishing skills with another work which commenced in Moneyslane, Co. Down. This work got under way, on the human level, out of missions and rallies he had conducted. Soon there was a flourishing congregation. A building fund was opened, a building programme was undertaken, and a new church building was opened in 1970. Meanwhile John Douglas had been busily engaged developing the spiritual side of the ministry there. Organising the Sunday School. Teaching the Scriptures. Preaching the Gospel, conducting numerous evangelistic campaigns — locally, as well as in different parts of the country.

God really blessed the ministry of John Douglas in the early 1970's. In addition to his responsibilities in Moneyslane, he undertook missions in America and Australia.

In late 1975, John received a call to the ministry of the Free Presbyterian Church in Lisburn. The most difficult part about accepting that call proved to be the breaking of the news to the congregation in Moneyslane. It was hard to come to terms with having to leave dear friends, although he had already been through something of the same kind of an experience when leaving Portavogie.

In January 1976, Rev. John Douglas took charge of Lisburn Free Presbyterian Church. And there was much to be done. Gradually the work began to grow and develop until the congregation itself became established. The debt was cleared on the property and on the new manse which had been erected.

In addition to his ministerial duties, John was soon to take on further responsibility. For a number of years he had been involved in the training of new ministers for the work of the church, so in 1979 he was ideally qualified to take up the position of Principal of the newly-established Whitefield College of the Bible.

This College, whose aim was to continue to provide theological training for the prospective ministers of the church, and then extended its courses to prepare young people for involvement in evangelism, ministry and children's work, was originally located in premises in Cyprus Avenue, Belfast. Owing to the steadily-rising demand for places, however, it was soon discovered that this site was too small. Too restrictive. There was no scope for expansion. So, in 1981 the College was moved to Lawrencetown, Co. Down. This tranquil rural setting by the River Bann, proved to be an ideal site. Quiet. Undisturbed. Conducive to study. Meditation and preparation.

Places in the College have always been in constant demand, and a high degree of success has been achieved amongst the students, most of whom become active in full-time work for the Lord in some capacity.

John Douglas often looks back and around, reflecting upon all the wonderful ways in which God has both led him and used him throughout his life. As he thinks of his resident ministry in three churches, his work as Clerk of Presbytery of the Free Presbyterian Church and the ever-demanding position as Principal of the Whitefield College of the Bible, his mind often travels back to the September Sunday when he first heard the promise of Jesus, "Him that cometh to me , I will in no wise cast out".

He came. And proved the promise to be true.

Jesus didn't cast him out.

And He hasn't let him down either, in all those years.

Not even once.

2

MR. RICO'S CIRCUS

❖

I t was a Thursday evening in June, 1948. The setting sun covered
the city of Belfast with its golden glow and cast giant stretchy
shadows across the Ravenhill Road.

Rev. Ian Paisley was walking home, up the road, from the prayer
meeting in Ravenhill Evangelical Mission Church, when he spotted a
large tent, just inside the gates of the Ormeau Park. The pennants
flying from the tops of the three main poles, and the banner across the
tent doorway, announced to all who were remotely interested that
Rico's Circus had come to town.

The preacher, who was always ready to seize any opportunity to
preach the Gospel, said to himself, "I would love to have a go at
preaching in that tent. They are going full steam ahead in there
tonight, but I will ask about it tomorrow."

So, next morning, as he had promised himself, he arrived down
amongst the higgledy-piggledy assortment of cages and caravans. The
circus 'complex'.

He asked for Mr. Rico. A circus hand said, "I will find him for you, sir."

Very shortly, a wee man emerged from one of the caravans. He was of Mediterranean appearance. Spanish or Italian, perhaps. He certainly wasn't from Belfast.

As the circus owner approached the big man who towered above him, he introduced himself. "I am Mr. Rico," he volunteered.

"And I am Ian Paisley," the preacher returned.

"Your reverence, what can I do for you?" the dapper little boss-man enquired.

Rev. Paisley went straight to the point, without any preamble. "I would like you to give me the chance to preach in your tent," he replied.

"That is interesting, because one of the English bishops preached in that tent," Mr. Rico observed, grinning broadly. "So if he preached in it, it should be all right for you, sir. If you can obtain permission to use it on Sunday night, you can have it. They wouldn't let me hold my circus in it on a Sunday night, but they may allow you to preach in it. I don't know."

He paused for breath, and the would-be-tent-preacher interrupted him, "I think I can get permission to use it O.K." he said, confidently.

"Very good, then. Very good!" Mr. Rico was so helpful. "I will announce that you will be speaking, here in my tent, on Sunday evening. I will announce it at every performance between now and then."

So the opportunist evangelist had procured, in one brief interview with one little man, free use of a large tent, with free advertising thrown in!

As he had anticipated, being granted permission to use the tent on the Sunday night didn't prove to be a problem. Rev. Paisley approached one of the city aldermen, who informed him, "The Sunday ban only applies to a circus performance. Not a Christian meeting. Preach away."

Ian Paisley didn't need to be told that twice! 'Preach away' is precisely what he did.

When it came to Sunday evening, the circus tent was packed. Over one thousand people crammed on to the tiers of seats ranged around 'the big top'. This was something of a novelty for both circus-lovers and church-goers alike. So they all turned out in force!

Four prominent local Christians each gave their testimony at the commencement of the unusual service, and then the fiery twenty-two year old preached, standing on a little makeshift platform, erected beside the circus ring. Ian Paisley was ringmaster that night, but he had no whip. Just his sword. The sword of the Spirit, which is the Word of God.

While the young minister faithfully presented the claims of the Gospel, his voice echoing around the tent, out through the canvas, across the Ormeau Park, and down the Ravenhill Road, the circus boss himself, the kindly Mr. Rico, stood below the platform. Throughout the entire meeting!

When he had finished speaking, Rev. Paisley appealed for seeking souls to come forward. "I feel God is dealing with some souls here tonight," he began. "So as our heads are bowed and our eyes are closed, just make your way round the tent to the front of the platform here, and someone will speak to you. Just come, not to Ian Paisley, but to Jesus. Some of you have heard the Gospel many times, yet you still haven't come to the Saviour. You can come to Him now. Here. Tonight. In this tent. And there may be others here who have never heard the glad news of the Gospel before. This is your first time. You, too, can come tonight. God loves you, Christ has died for you, and now He is calling you. Just come..."

And they came.

Slowly, a number of people made their way forward to the front. Convinced of their need of salvation, convicted by the Holy Spirit of God, they stood silently, reverently, wanting to be saved.

One of those who blessed God for Ian Paisley's burden to preach in Mr. Rico's tent was Ida, the daughter of an elder in the Ravenhill Evangelical Mission Church. Ida had been to many Gospel services, had heard many solemn messages, and yet she still wasn't saved.

That night she came forward to the front of the tent, was counselled, and put her faith in Christ. Ida is still praising God for Mr. Rico and his circus tent...

For Ian Paisley and his impulsive spiritual vision...

And for the wonderful Saviour, Master and Friend, whom she came to know one balmy summer evening.

3

RISE UP AND GO

❖

It is amazing how God intervenes in the lives of people. Some times those who are least expecting any kind of Divine intervention.

Such was the experience of young Hazel Miskimmin.

Throughout her childhood years Hazel had been influenced by many who had faithfully taught her the truths of the Gospel. She had four saved aunts, and a number of dedicated Sunday School teachers. Even when evacuated to Ballymena during the Second World War she spent a year in the class of a Christian schoolteacher who was concerned not only for his pupils' secular education, but also for their spiritual welfare.

Perhaps the most permanent and consistent witness to her, however, was that of her saved and caring mother.

After the War the Miskimmin family moved house in Belfast, and Hazel renewed her friendship with a girl whom she hadn't seen since they were both only three years of age. This girl became Hazel's closest friend. They really enjoyed each other's company, and advanced into teenage together. Hazel and her friend were often invited along to Gospel meetings and missions. Especially by one of her friend's neighbours in Rusholme Street, off Agnes Street. This lady had been saved at a campaign in the Keswick Street Mission, and had a burning desire to see others brought to the Saviour.

In October, 1947, the two chums had a squabble. They fell out. About something stupid and petty. And after a few days each of them regretted it, but who was going to make the first move towards reconciliation? Break the ice. Climb down.

Then one Friday night a young boy arrived at Hazel's door. It was her friend's brother, with a little bit of crumpled up paper in his hand. Hazel opened the piece of paper when he gave it over to her, and it turned out to be a note from her friend suggesting that they both go together to a meeting in Keswick Street Mission Hall.

Hazel was delighted to receive that invitation. She recognised it as an olive branch. Strand One in the peace process. So she accepted.

It would be just great to have an evening out with her best friend again. Wherever they were.

Keswick Street Mission had once been a wine shop, but when it closed and then lay vacant for a while, Joe Anderson of Tennant Street, a member of Shankill Road Baptist Church, rented it. His reason for doing this was to see his friends and neighbours reached with the glad news of the Gospel. The mission was his life's investment.

The little room was packed with local people when the two chums went in. They found a place where they could sit side by side. How wonderful just to be together again.

It was all very bright and cheery. The singing was lively and enthusiastic. The room itself had all been done up in warm colours. Everybody who was there seemed to be happy to be there. Hazel was just deciding that she could probably spend an hour in there O.K. when the door of the little prayer room at the back opened and out stooped the tallest, lankiest man she had ever seen! 'What a big drink of water!' she thought.

And the height of him was nothing in comparison to the sound that came out when he opened his mouth. His voice boomed out like thunder, reverberating round the little room. The two friends almost jumped out of their skins. But they also sat up and took notice.

When Rev. Ian Paisley got up to speak he began by announcing his text, inviting everyone to 'turn it up' in their Bibles. Hazel had her Bible with her but she sat on it, hiding it in the folds of her skirt.

She didn't think that she was going to be at all interested in what the reading was anyway. She was there in body, but not in spirit. Out for the night to make it up with her friend.

The verse the preacher read over twice, in his resonant voice, was Proverbs 29 v 1. "He, that being often reproved hardeneth his neck, shall suddenly be destroyed, and that without remedy."

Those words went straight to the heart of young Hazel Miskimmin.

'Being often reproved. Hardening her neck'. And her heart. That was her. All summed up...

From somewhere God's hammer struck. Smashing her careless, carefree attitude all to pieces in one mighty blow.

And the sword of the Spirit pierced her soul...

It was not of herself. She had no interest in the things of God, no ears for the Word of God, and up until that night, no desire whatsoever to be saved...

'Being often reproved. Hardening her neck'.

This was a word of rebuke. And there was a word of warning, too. 'Shall suddenly be destroyed, and that without remedy.'

Hazel's mind travelled back to her aunts, and all their genuine care for her spiritual welfare. Then there were all those challenging Gospel messages that she had heard in her childhood. And the times that she would have liked to be saved. But put it off.

Surely she must be the person of Proverbs 29...

The sword of the Spirit had plunged deep into her soul and the battle was on. She could no longer remain indifferent to the powerful challenge of God's Word.

As the meeting progressed, Hazel couldn't remember all that the big preacher said, but she was aware that he repeated John chapter 3 v16 a time or two. She knew that verse well. Off by heart, in fact. Her mind flashed back to the times when, as a very young child she was placed up on a table or a chair, during week-end visits to her Grandmother Miskimmin's home, and asked to do her party piece. Say 'For God so loved the world...' or 'The Lord is my shepherd...' for all the guests present.

However, with all her head knowledge of John 3 v 16, Hazel had never been able to appreciate how God's loving sacrifice applied to her as an individual. After all, was she not just an insignificant speck compared with all the hundreds, thousands and millions of the world's population represented at Calvary?

As the meeting drew to a close God's servant continued to plead with the hardened hearts present. He made an earnest appeal for 'souls to come to Christ.'

"As our heads are bowed," he began, "is there somebody in the gathering who isn't going to put the Saviour off any longer? Some young person, perhaps who is going to respond to His love?.."

For Hazel the voice soon became a drone in the distance. Like an aeroplane far away, and going away. She was engaged in her own personal battle. Her own mental struggle. God had given her a vision of Calvary. Of Jesus dying there for her. She saw, for the first time, that Christ was bearing HER sins on that cross... And she wanted desperately to respond to His love. And His call. But then there was also the call of the world. She was dead scared that she was going to miss something if she came to Christ. And she was conscious of how rebellious her heart had often been. Would the Saviour still want her, even if she did come to Him now, she wondered?

Suddenly she was roused from her reverie by a noise beside her.

She opened one eye, just half.

And what she saw goaded her into action.

Her friend was on her feet.

When she had found her own, and the strength to stand on them, Hazel stood up beside her. It was now or never, she felt.

Later, in the little prayer room at the back, the two friends sat side by side, as Rev. Ian Paisley read a number of Scripture texts to them. Hazel recognised many of them from her younger days. A number of them, like Romans chapter 10 and verse 9 she knew off by heart.

Sitting there in that tiny room that evening, Hazel Miskimmin, aged fifteen, simply trusted in Christ as her Saviour. And much to her delight, her friend was also saved as well.

It was Friday, 27th October, 1947.

Hazel was so happy, so excited, and yet so content, on the way home. She wasn't long into the house, either, until she told her mother that she had got saved.

Mrs. Miskimmin was overjoyed. What an answer to prayer!

It was two months later, in December, that Hazel was first challenged with the possibility of serving the Lord in a full-time capacity. Somehow. Somewhere.

A group of Americans had come to conduct a Christmas service in the Albert Hall Mission on the Shankill Road. Hazel and some more of an ever-widening circle of Christian friends went along. How they enjoyed the evening! It was really wonderful! Hazel loved the warmth and zeal of the American team.

It was all so cosy.

Cosy, that was, until the challenge at the end. It really burnt into her soul.

One of the team leaders asked quite simply, and very directly, "If the Lord should call you to serve him as a missionary in some foreign land, would you be ready and willing to go?"

Those words hit home.

Since her conversion, Hazel had been all fired up with spiritual enthusiasm. She was just going to do marvellous things for God. After all, hadn't He done marvellous things for her? She thought she was ready to do anything, or go anywhere, for her new Master. But was she?

When Hazel began to consider all that was involved in going to the mission field, she began to have second thoughts.

It would mean leaving the security and warmth of a loving family. She wasn't ready to do that, she reckoned. Not in the meantime, anyway.

It would also mean leaving all her friends, none of whom, it seemed, were as keen to serve God as she was. And that would be a big thing. For she loved them all very much, and they were having great times together.

Another thing that rather tempered her enthusiasm was the thought of undergoing preparatory training for the mission field in a Bible College or some such place. Hazel had never been particularly fond of school and against her parents wishes had withdrawn from the Business Training course at Belfast Mercantile College. So the prospect of returning to full-time study didn't exactly send her into ecstasies.

She was, in fact, actually anything but ready and willing to go. So she stayed at home.

In the few years that followed that October night in 1947, Hazel enjoyed her Christian life. She had so many like-minded friends. They all travelled together to youth rallies and Faith Mission conferences. It was terrific!

But still Hazel tried to shut her mind to the challenge of missionary work. She didn't like to hear anybody reading or speaking about Romans chapter 12. It was all about 'presenting your body a living sacrifice, wholly acceptable unto God'. She tried to plug her ears to that kind of ministry now.

There was no escaping the call of God, however.

The Keswick Street Mission were a very missionary-minded group. They had a genuine concern for the souls of men and women, boys and girls, worldwide.

It was hardly surprising, then, that when a man called John Cupples had a mission there, he presented the missionary challenge very earnestly to the Saturday night Youth Fellowship. At the end of the meeting he asked for a show of hands of those who would be willing to go and serve the Lord on the mission field, should He call them. And he waited. And waited. And waited.

Nobody or nothing stirred.

Not a single hand was raised.

Hazel felt miserable. She really wanted to be of some use to God. But she just hadn't the courage of her convictions. To go it alone.

After the Youth Fellowship a good number of the young people congregated in a friend's house.

One of the ladies present, a neighbour of their hostess, and a member of the Keswick Street Mission, had something to say to them all. Something that was weighing heavily on her mind.

"See you young people", she stormed, "I was ashamed of the whole job-lot of you there tonight! There wasn't even one of you interested in serving God!"

While some of the others made excuses for themselves, Hazel sat in the silence of conscience. Ashamed and miserable.

To salve her conscience she decided to give generous financial support to foreign missions. If she wouldn't go to the mission field she could at least support those who did. It would always be something, she felt. Even though it was only a half-way measure.

In 1953, Hazel, by then almost twenty-one years of age, attended the Faith Mission Easter Convention in Hamilton Road Presbyterian Church, Bangor. The theme of the Convention that year was 'One Hundred Per Cent For God'. The speaker was Dr. Alan Redpath.

Hazel was intrigued to hear that great man of God confess that he had once heard the call of God to go and witness to "China's millions". He hadn't obeyed that call and now he reckoned that what he was doing, which was wonderful in some people's eyes, was only a very poor "second-best".

At the close of the conference a very powerful challenge was presented. Was there anybody, but anybody, who was willing to give their lives to the service of God, at home or on the mission field?

Here it was again. Another spiritual crisis for Hazel.

This time there could be no putting it off. No excuses and no holding back.

She stood to her feet...

After the Easter Holidays Hazel returned to work. She was a supervisor in a shirt factory.

One day she was chatting to a Christian friend in the factory. As they discussed all that had happened over the holiday period, Hazel told Iris about the Convention. And her commitment.

"And what are you going to do now then, Hazel?" her friend enquired.

"What do you mean, 'What are you going to do now?'. I don't know what I'm going to do. What do you think I should do?" Hazel replied.

There was silence for a second or two, then her friend went on, "I'm not awful sure what you should do, but I do know this, you can't stand up in a meeting like that and then just do nothing. You must do SOMETHING."

That made Hazel think. It was dead right. She would have to do something. And she did.

She went to see William Mc Comb, from the Acre Gospel Mision. He listened to her story, and, recognising in her a young woman who had a tremendous potential for God, he recommended that she do two things. Prepare for missionary service in two different ways. Vocationally and spiritually. Train as a nurse or a teacher, and attend Bible College.

It was all a bit daunting to someone who had never been all that keen on 'book-learning'. But she had pledged herself to God and to His work. She had now come to the point of committing her 'body a living sacrifice to God'. And she would go through with it.

So, in September, 1953, Hazel left the shirt factory and entered Belfast City Hospital where she trained as a nurse, and then as a mid-wife. After working for a short period in the hospital to gain experience she then turned her attentions to equipping herself spiritually for missionary work.

She enrolled in Swansea Bible College.

Then, in July, 1961, Hazel sailed for Brazil, under the auspices of the Acre Gospel Mission, and in the care of James and Dorrie Gunning. It was there, in that vast South American country, that she spent the next thirty years of her life, faithfully serving the God she loves.

That, however, is a story in itself.

4

THE UNPARDONABLE SIN?

---------------- ❖ ----------------

People crammed into the evening services in Ravenhill Evangelical Mission Church in the late 1940's and early 50's. Every Sunday the place was packed. They came to hear a fiery preacher, in his mid-twenties, called Rev. Ian Paisley. The preaching of this forthright young minister was causing quite a stir amongst the people of the city, and God was causing quite a stir amongst the people who came to hear him. Souls were being saved every week.

One particular Sunday evening, late in the autumn of 1951, a smart looking late-teenage girl made her way into the enquiry room after a service when Rev. Paisley had preached the Gospel, and then made an appeal. In those days a young woman called Eileen Cassells was one of the church counsellors, and Rev. Paisley liked her. He trusted her spiritual wisdom and insight so much that he relied upon her to deal with ladies in the enquiry room, when possible.

So Eileen sat down beside the girl, who couldn't have been more than seventeen. Two things about her impressed the would-be counsellor. The first was the way in which she was dressed. And the second was the way in which she was distressed.

The girl was wearing a neat suit and blouse with a matching hat. A really fashionable outfit. She didn't look out of place in her surroundings. Indeed, she conformed to the dress code exactly. Looked as though she belonged.

Trouble was, but, that she didn't. And it seemed to be upsetting her. She appeared distraught. Silent tears flowed down a very pretty face.

"What's the matter ?" Eileen enquired, softly, not really knowing how to begin, with someone in such a state.

"I don't think I can ever be saved !" the girl blurted out, her voice trembling.

"And what makes you think that ?" Eileen went on. Probing.

The girl hesitated. It was obvious to the counsellor that she had a deep, dark secret hidden somewhere at the roots of her being. They both sat in silence for a few minutes. The girl wiped away her tears with a dainty lace handkerchief. Slowly. Deliberately. Gave her precious thinking time.

When she did decide to tell the whole story, it all came out in a torrent. Like a lock-gate opening.

"I have done a terrible thing", she said, hastily. It was get-it-over-with-time now. "Some people are even saying it is the unpardonable sin. A lot of my friends don't want anything more to do with me now. And they are saying horrible things about me behind my back. I feel so awful. So lonely..."

Patience was required.

The truth was coming.

Eileen felt so sorry for the girl who was only a couple of years younger than herself. Instinctively, she put an arm around her.

"The fact is that I had a baby four months ago, and I'm not married," she sobbed. "Everybody is down on me. I must be the worst sinner that ever lived. I feel like an outcast. Unclean. Like a leper."

When Eileen knew 'the fact', then she could begin to console. To comfort. And to counsel.

"That is not the unpardonable sin," she began, tenderly. "God still loves you, and He still wants to save you. Jesus will still forgive your sins. And take them away."

As the girl listened intently, Eileen told her the story of the woman in the Bible, who had been caught committing adultery. She ended with the compassionate words of the Saviour, "Neither do I condemn thee ; go, and sin no more". (John 8 v 11)

The gloom seemed to lift from the face of the teenage mother. When she realised that she wasn't the only one who had ever sinned, and that there was still some sort of hope for her, she brightened considerably.

"Are you trying to tell me that I can still be saved?" she asked.

"That's exactly what I am trying to tell you," her counsellor assured her.

"Well can I be saved now? Here?" was the next question.

"Indeed you can," Eileen was only too happy to tell her.

"I want to be saved, then," she replied, eagerly.

After Eileen had explained how that God, in His love, had given His only Son to die on the cross to take away her sin, both young women knelt down at a seat. And the seeking, sorrowing soul simply accepted the Saviour. She was saved.

As they rose, a few moments later, the girl's face was shining. "I just can't believe it!" she exclaimed. "I feel so unburdened. The weight has gone."

"And what's more, it has gone for good," Eileen added." For God says, 'Your sins and iniquities will I remember no more.'"

That girl left that meeting that evening, saved, happy, and ready to rebuild her life on a strong foundation. She was glad that she hadn't committed the unpardonable sin. And the ones she had committed were 'gone for good'...

What a wonderful, comforting concept!

She went on her way rejoicing. Looking to God for the future.

Then on 13th October, 1956, the counsellor married the minister. Miss Eileen Cassells became Mrs. Ian Paisley. And they also went on their way rejoicing. Looking to God for the future.

5

THE HIDE-AND-SEEK BIBLE

❖

When he was eighteen years of age, Jack Davidson, who had been living in Cookstown, obtained employment in Belfast, and came to live in the city. And there he met Clara Feely.

After they had been 'going together' for four years, Jack and Clara were married in 1939. The newly-weds set up home in Frenchpark Street, one of a maze of little streets, running off the Donegall Road, near to the Royal Victoria Hospital.

Soon after they were married, The Second World War broke out, and Jack became an ambulance driver in the city.

Belfast was strategic because of its shipbuilding yards and aircraft factories. So it became a prime target for enemy bombs.

After being out for nights and days at a time Jack used to come home very upset. And tell Clara harrowing tales of what he had seen.

Blazing buildings. Battered buildings. And big holes in the road where buildings used to be.

Mangled mounds of humanity.

Some were only slightly injured. Some had horrific, maiming injuries.

And there were many, many dead.

During the worst of the blitz, Clara was evacuated from Belfast, out into the country. She went to stay with an aunt in Lawrencetown, near Banbridge, Co. Down, and it was while she was there that Jack and Clara's first child, John, was born.

When the War ended, in 1945, Clara moved back to Belfast, to Frenchpark Street. And to be with Jack again.

As the work for the emergency ambulance service had come to an end, Jack needed another job. And with the help of Clara's father, who worked at the docks, he found one. As a docker. Working on the boats as they came and went from Belfast's busy harbour.

It may have been a good thing for Jack to be in employment again, and reasonably well paid employment at that, but the move to the docks wasn't altogether a marvellous boon to everybody, in every way.

For it was at the docks, and with his mates, the dockers, that Jack began to frequent the local public houses. And drink. Heavily.

Things deteriorated so badly, so quickly, that it soon came to the stage that Jack hardly ever came home on a Friday or Saturday night, sober. And when drinking, or drunk, he seemed to become a totally different person.

At home, and sober, during the week, Jack Davidson was very kind. And very fussy. He often helped to clean around the little family home, and it used to give him great pleasure to 'polish the brasses'. Sparkling brass was his pride and joy.

No matter what happened, either, he always insisted upon taking Clara and the family away for a holiday in the summer. This could prove quite a problem for him, financially, as by that time they had four children. John had been joined by a brother, Lawrence, and two sisters, Gail and Heather.

The fact that he spent so much of his earnings on drink, made an ever difficult financial burden almost impossible. But Jack managed.

He borrowed the money to take them all away in the summer. Then spent all winter paying it back!

Jack was a fanatical football fan. A Linfield supporter. A 'Blues' man. And he went along to all of their matches. Never missed a one, if he could help it

If Linfield won their match, Jack and his fellow supporters went along to the pub for a drink. To celebrate. And Jack got drunk.

And if Linfield should happen to have lost the match, Jack and his fellow supporters went along to the pub for a drink. To 'drown their sorrows'. And Jack got drunk.

So any which way, Jack Davidson ended up drunk. Nearly every Saturday night.

Thus Clara and the family never really looked forward to the weekends. Friday night was pay night. Saturday night was match night. And on either, or both, of those nights, Jack was likely to arrive home intoxicated.

On the occasions when he actually made it into the house, he used to lie on the floor, unlace his boots, with great difficulty, and kick them off. And he didn't care where they landed, either. Or what they smashed. Distressing for a wife, trying to keep a tidy home. For himself, as well, when he returned to his senses.

Sometimes he just never made it into the house. He often tripped over a step in the yard. And lay there. Or sat huddled up in the outside toilet. Until sober. If the night was rough, and some member of the family was feeling kind, they threw a rug or blanket over him, and he lay there until he came round.

If Clara came upon him, with half-full bottles in his pocket, she confiscated the bottles and poured the remaining contents down a drain. That meant that she wasn't altogether Jack's most popular person, when he discovered his loss.

In short, it wasn't the recipe for a blissful marriage.

Although Jack was often drunk, he never failed to give Clara the weekly grocery allowance, which was never enough to feed a growing family. She had to do a lot of skimping and saving, to feed and clothe them all.

There was one winter's night that Jack came home, inebriated, and put Clara and little Heather, just five years old, out into the snow. "If you don't get out and leave me alone, I'm going to burn this house down!" he yelled at them.

Clara knew that he was capable of it. So out they went.

Over an hour later they crept back.

Husband-and-father was asleep, as they suspected he would be. Everything had calmed down. Until the next time.

Often, when he sobered up, late on a Sunday afternoon, after spending the most of the day in bed, Jack Davidson regretted his drunken exploits. As he searched the docks area for his old bike, which he could never ride, so he usually left it behind him, after a drinking session, he wondered what it was all about.

Yet still he didn't stop.

In the mid-1950's, something happened which had more of an effect on Jack, and his life, than he cared to admit at the time.

Clara got saved.

Rev. John Girvan, who was assistant minister in Richview Presbyterian Church, had planned to visit the Davidson household in the course of his ministerial duties. One night, at about ten o'clock, he was led by God, from another home, to call with Clara. As he read from the Bible the words from Genesis chapter six, 'My spirit shall not always strive with man,' the mother-of-four was convicted. She realized that it was time that she trusted the Saviour.

So Clara did that, sitting in her own living-room, Jack out, and the children in bed.

When she told her husband of her conversion, on one of his calm and caring days, he said he was pleased. And to prove it he bought her a Bible. A very acceptable and wholly appropriate gesture.

When the other Jack Davidson surfaced, however, in a fit of drunkenness, spite or bad temper, at the weekend, he used to hide the Bible, so that she couldn't find it!

Then on a Monday or Tuesday morning it would miraculously reappear!

It became the hide-and-seek Bible!

New life in Christ brought with it, for Clara Davidson, a new desire to see others, and particularly her own husband and family, brought to Him. How she longed to see them experience the peace of soul that she had found since she had trusted the Saviour.

So she did what she could about it. She began to pray for them all. Both in private, and in a little women's prayer group.

Four other women joined Clara in her home in Frenchpark Street, once a week, when Jack was at work. Not to gossip or drink tea. They weren't just there to while away an hour or two. They had a clearly defined aim.

It was to pray.

They met to pray for their husbands, their families, and their friends.

However, since all of Clara's prayer partners were aware of her home situation, one of their chief petitions was, "Lord, save Jack. And change him. For only You can do it!"

It was on every woman's lips. Every week.

Then, after a series of bad weekends, someone spoke to Rev. Girvan, and let him know how tough things were becoming for Clara. She was trying to do her best for her family, and maintain a consistent Christian testimony, with an often-drunk and usually totally unsympathetic husband.

Rev. Girvan called with Clara one day and told her that he was considering paying Jack a visit some time. Although she appreciated the kind minister's genuine concern, Clara wasn't convinced that his plan to visit Jack was one of his best-ever ideas.

Jack could be short-tempered. And he was certainly, physically, very strong.

What would happen if he lost his temper and landed the reverend gentleman out on the street? What on earth would the neighbours think, then?

However, Rev. Girvan persisted, a date was agreed, and he called to see Jack Davidson.

Much to Clara's surprise, and complete relief, her husband was very mild, when they met. Unusually subdued, indeed, when Rev. Girvan read the Scriptures with them.

The passage that he read had obviously been chosen carefully, thoughtfully, in advance. It was Luke 17 vs 1 and 2. No wonder Jack sat sheepishly, as he heard...

'Then said he unto the disciples, It is impossible but that offences will come: but woe unto him through whom they come!

It were better for him that a millstone were hanged about his neck, and he cast into the sea, than that he should offend one of these little ones...'

Strong, pointed, stuff. It must have made an impression on Jack, too.

For he tried to reform. Tried to cut down on 'the bottle'.

But it only lasted for a week or two.

Then he was back. As bad as ever. Again.

Another interest which Jack had, outside of work, and in addition to his fervent following of Linfield Football Club, was his membership of the Orange Order and The Royal Black Institution. And it was through his association with these organisations that he first heard Rev. Ian Paisley speaking.

He was lying in bed one Sunday morning, early in 1964, sleeping off the effects of the night before, as usual, when he remembered that there was to be a big Covenant Commemoration Service that day, addressed by Rev. Paisley.

On first hearing of that service Jack had promised himself, "I will go to that one when it comes around. I won't miss it."

Now the day had come. So Jack kept his promise to himself. He went along.

Throughout his life, Jack Davidson had always admired men who weren't afraid to say what they thought. Especially so when what they said was what he would have said himself.

He liked sincere, honest people, and when he heard Rev. Ian Paisley preach in that service that day, he recognised such a person right away.

A man who had the courage of his convictions.

A man who seemed to know what he was talking about.

And a man who wasn't a bit afraid to confront his audience with the truth of the Gospel.

On his way home from that Covenant Commemoration Service in the Ulster Hall, Jack made himself a further promise. "I will go and hear that man preaching, in his own church next Sunday," he resolved.

On the very next Sunday, Clara was pleased to see her husband dress himself up to go out to Church. What a stir that would cause amongst the prayer group when they heard of it!

Unfortunately, however, when Jack arrived at Ravenhill Free Presbyterian Church, the doors were shut. Closed firmly. He couldn't get in! So many people were already packed into the building that the stewards had no choice but to close the doors. There wasn't room for another single person. And Jack was outside.

On his way home he vowed that he would return on the next Sunday night.

So, much to the delight of Clara and her praying friends, Jack left a bit earlier on the following Sunday evening to cross the city to Ravenhill Free Presbyterian Church. But again it was the same story. Church crammed. Doors closed. He couldn't be allowed in.

On his way home, on that second shut-out Sunday night, he determined that he wanted to hear Ian Paisley preach, as obviously did hundreds of others. He would go really early next Sunday night. To hear Rev. Paisley preach the Gospel.

And he did that.

At the third attempt, Jack Davidson gained admittance to Ravenhill Free Presbyterian Church, and it was only when he was inside that he realized why the doors had been closed on the previous nights. As indeed they had been that night, too.

Every available seat in the church was taken. People were crushed together into every available space in the building. Even the steps up to the platform served as seats for some of the younger men.

When Rev. Paisley began to preach, Jack Davidson hung upon his every word. After all, he had waited four weeks for this! He wasn't long listening to that message, though, until Jack got beyond the man on the platform. For although Jack admired the speaker's stance on many issues, he forgot completely about his dynamic personality or his political dogma that night.

The Holy Spirit was at work in his soul.

He wanted to be saved.

At the end of the service, the preacher appealed for anybody who was in earnest about being saved to come forward to the enquiry room at the rear of the church.

One of the first up out of his seat and into the enquiry room was Jack Davidson. He had only heard the Gospel a few times. But he had a wife who was saved. People who were praying for him. And a Saviour Who had died to take away his sins. Which were many, he knew.

There could be no doubt about it. He was in earnest to be saved.

And in that enquiry room, in March, 1964, in tears, as Rev. Paisley read some verses from the Bible to him, and explained God's way of salvation very simply, Jack Davidson came to faith in Christ.

What rejoicing when he arrived home, and told Clara what had happened!

What a revelation to him, also! It was only then that he discovered the volume of prayer that had gone up to God for him. Clara and her Christian friends had been praying for his salvation, both collectively and individually, for nearly ten years!

What a change in Jack's life, too. His drinking pals just couldn't understand what had happened to him. But they thought he would soon be 'back on the bottle' with them. 'Jack Davidson will never stay good-living,' they prophesied. But they were to be proved wrong. Not that Jack had any power within himself to 'stay good-living'.

God, though, had the power to keep him. And demonstrated it.

The transition in Jack's life made a big change in the home, and in the neighbourhood. Family, friends and neighbours all recognised that Jack was different. God had worked a marvellous miracle in his life.

For a while after Jack was saved, Clara still continued to attend Richview Presbyterian Church, refusing Jack's invitations to go along with him to hear Rev. Paisley. She wasn't sure if she would like to be in one of 'that big man's meetings'. Thought he might just be 'a bit loud', for her liking...

Then, to please Jack, who was really 'a new man', and so full of praise for the minister of Ravenhill Free Presbyterian Church, she gave in, and went along with him to 'his church' on a Sunday evening, late in the summer of 1964.

It wasn't long after hearing him for that first time that Clara was travelling over with her husband, every Sunday, to hear Rev. Paisley preaching. There were three things about the man who had led Jack to the Lord, that Clara found she liked. His forthright style, his undeniable sincerity, and above all, his unquestionable grasp of the fundamentals of the Gospel.

A few years after his conversion, organisers from Church groups around Belfast, and across Northern Ireland, began to invite Jack to 'give his testimony'. Tell how he came to Christ. It was such an absorbing story.

Although he was a very strong man, physically, Jack was naturally very shy. It always took a lot of gentle coaxing to persuade him to take the platform.

But when he did, it was great!

Audiences were enthralled by the docker whose life had been so radically changed when he was saved. Jack was living proof of what God could do for somebody who was willing to trust Him.

When telling of his experience of conversion, Jack Davidson invariably did two things. They became an essential part of his 'programme'.

The first was that he read from Ephesians chapter 2, explaining to his listeners that after he was saved he searched the Bible for some reference to a situation and condition like his. When he came upon Ephesians chapter 2, he realized that he had found it.

In those verses he discovered himself depicted. Exactly. What he was. And what he had become.

After reading aloud the first three verses, telling what his life had been like in the past, Jack often drew attention to the 'But', of verse four.

'BUT God, who is rich in mercy, for his great love wherewith he loved us,'.

He then continued reading the next three verses, which, he said, described what God had done for him...

'Even when we were dead in sins, hath quickened us together with Christ, (by grace ye are saved;)

And hath raised us up together, and made us sit together in heavenly places in Christ Jesus:

That in the ages to come he might shew the exceeding riches of his grace in his kindness toward us through Christ Jesus...'

When concluding his testimony, Jack usually sang for his audiences. Again, what he sang, was a hymn that for him, summarised his whole life story. He emphasized the last line of each verse, particularly. It portrayed precisely his condition before conversion, he said. 'A poor sinner'.

People were moved to tears as Jack Davidson sang, with deep feeling :-

I was once far away from the Saviour,
As vile as a sinner could be,
And I wondered if Christ the Redeemer
Could save a poor sinner like me.

I wandered alone in the darkness,
Not a ray of light could I see,
And the thought filled my heart with sadness,
There's no hope for a sinner like me.

And then in the dark lonely hour,
A voice sweetly whispered to me,
Saying, "Christ the Redeemer hath power,
To save a poor sinner like thee."

I listened and lo! 'twas the Saviour
That was speaking so kindly to me,
And I cried, "I'm the chief of sinners,
Canst thou save a poor sinner like me?"

Then fully I trusted in Jesus,
And oh! now a joy came to me;
My heart was filled with His praises,
For saving a sinner like me.

No longer in darkness I'm walking,
The light is now shining on me,
And now unto others I'm telling
How he saved a poor sinner like me.

For just over twenty years, from that Sunday in March, 1964, when Jack came to personal faith in Jesus Christ, he and Clara lived happily together. Often reading, and discussing, the Word of God with each other.

No hide-and-seek Bibles now!

And it was Jack's chief delight to tell others of how God had 'saved a poor sinner' like him.

Then, one morning in May, 1984, Jack was up and around as usual. And he said to his wife as they prepared for yet another day together, "Clara, I have a wee promise for you for today. I was just reading it there. It's this, 'Casting all your care upon him. For he careth for you.'"

A few minutes later, Jack went into the front room of the pensioner's bungalow, to which they had moved, from Frenchpark Street. 'To do the fire.'

When Clara thought that it was taking him unusually long, and that he was doing his job unusually quietly, she went in to check on him.

And she found her husband, Jack, curled up on the floor, at the fireplace, dead.

He had suffered a massive heart attack. And was gone.

His 'wee promise' for his wife had been his last words.

The suddenness of his passing was a tremendous shock for Clara, but for Jack, the last verse of the hymn that he had sung so often, with such genuine conviction, had become an instant reality...

And when life's journey is over,
And I the dear Saviour shall see,
I'll praise him for ever and ever
For saving a sinner like me.

Jack is in the Saviour's presence.
Praising Him for salvation.
Right now.

6

RIGHTFUL RECOGNITION

A s a teenager, Bill Woods had two main interests in his life, outside of home and school. The first was his membership of the Boy's Brigade, and the other his attendance, with his brother Bob, on the invitation of their cousin, Anne Robinson, to hear Rev. Ian Paisley preach, in his church on the Ravenhill Road. And both of these leisure-time pursuits were to prove instrumental in bringing about an important change in the young lad's life.

Bill loved the Boy's Brigade. He was a member of the 30th Belfast Company, based in Orangefield Presbyterian Church. The Company Captain was Fred Mc Cormick. 'Pop' the boys called him. Not only was 'Pop' diligent in supervising the moral and ethical instruction of the boys in his care, but he also longed that they would come to know Christ as Saviour, early in life.

When in his early teens, Bill started to attend the evening services in Ravenhill Free Presbyterian Church. This wasn't because he had any particular love for Church services on Sunday evenings.

But he did love to hear Rev. Paisley speak. He was different from anybody that he had ever heard before. The way he walked about and preached it out. So earnestly. So sincerely. He preached the Gospel because he was totally convinced that it was 'the power of God unto salvation.' And his fervour was infectious.

His church was always full.

It seemed that in every Sunday evening service, God blessed his preaching. Somebody was saved.

These two interests in Bill's life combined in a wonderful way, in July 1952, to see him led to faith in Christ.

In the middle of that month, Bill went to a Boy's Brigade camp in Kirkcaldy, Scotland. It was great fun. A real adventure. Sleeping out in tents. Playing games and visiting fascinating new places. But there was more to it than that.

At that camp, Bill was challenged directly with the claims of Christ. With the need to turn to Him for salvation. Although Bill heard the Gospel message at that camp, and was moved by it, he did nothing about it. Put off making any decision.

On the Sunday evening, after he had returned from Scotland, Bill went along to the evening service in Ravenhill Free Presbyterian Church. At that meeting, Rev. Paisley preached the Gospel with all his usual fire and enthusiasm. Bill was convicted. Yet again.

The appeal came at the end of the service. "As our heads are bowed, and the Christians are praying, I believe that God is speaking to some soul in the stillness," the speaker began. "That could be you. If it is, now is the time to come to Christ. Come as we are singing. If you make your way up to the front here, we will be delighted to talk to you. To counsel you. To point you to the Saviour..."

Bill was struggling with it. 'Do I really want to be saved? Now? Tonight? What will I tell my friends in school? They will make fun of me, I know. But then, this might be my last chance.' All kinds of thoughts reeled about in his mind.

Suddenly, he made the vital decision. Bill stood up, then made his way quietly forward to the enquiry room. He wanted to be saved. And he wasn't going to let another opportunity pass. In that little room at the back of the church, Mr. Jim Wetherall talked to the teenage lad, read some Bible verses with him, and pointed him to the Lord.

For a few weeks after that night, very few people knew that Bill had become a Christian. He didn't go about broadcasting it. He was either too shy, or too scared. Afraid of the ridicule of his friends at school. Or scared that he couldn't 'live up to it.' Or, perhaps, a bit of both.

New life, like the first signs of spring, couldn't be hidden, however. It began to burst out all over. The young convert began to take an interest in serious Bible study, and he loved to attend meetings of all sorts. Gospel meetings, teaching meetings, prayer meetings and missionary meetings...

Missionary meetings. That was where the future direction of young Bill Woods' life was determined. When he heard missionaries home on furlough tell of their labours for God in foreign lands, he was both inspired and challenged. Moved and motivated, all at once. How marvellous it must be to serve God like that! To preach the Gospel and teach the Word of God to people who had never ever heard the soul-saving life-changing message before.

After giving the matter constant and serious consideration, Bill decided that he wanted to devote his life to the work of the Lord. As a missionary.

So it was, that after a period of training in Bible College, Bill Woods, at nearly twenty-two years of age, set sail from Belfast harbour for Liverpool, where he boarded the liner, S.S. Hubert. He was on his way to Brazil, to serve God, in the jungles of the Amazon.

As Bill worked amongst the people of Brazil he soon recognised that they had two needs. First and foremost, they needed salvation. So he preached the Gospel and expounded the Scriptures at every opportunity.

There was also another, a more practical, need, which he identified. It was the need for medical help. As a missionary, in a remote area, he was so often confronted with sad cases where specialist medical help was required. He and his fellow missionaries did whatever they possibly could to relieve the suffering of the poor people whom they loved, and amongst whom they worked, but they were often left feeling hopelessly inadequate.

A conviction grew within Bill's thinking. He could be of so much more use to the Lord, and to the people of Brazil, if he had a medical qualification. If he was a doctor.

The gap between having bright ideas and putting them into practice is often wide. Some people think a lot but do very little. That wasn't the sort of Bill Woods. He was prepared to do something about the situation. So in 1968 he sat the entrance examination for the University of Amazonas, was successful, and in 1969 began his studies in the University's Medical School.

In the summer of 1974, after five years of intensive study, William John Woods graduated, top of his year group. He was now a fully qualified doctor. What was more, he was now fully equipped to serve God and the people of Brazil in a very practical fashion.

For over twenty years now, Bill has been involved in medical missionary work in that vast country, especially amongst leprosy patients. The nature and quality of his work has, on a number of occasions, been recognised by the Brazilian government. Perhaps the highest earthly recognition of his achievements came in November, 1997, when he was presented with the O.B.E., (Order of the British Empire), by Her Majesty The Queen, during an investiture ceremony at Buckingham Palace.

Bill himself, however, keeps labouring on for the Lord, striving towards an even higher, an even greater reward than that. It will be when his Heavenly Father recognises the nature and quality of his work, in a day still to come, with the simple words, "Well done, good and faithful servant."

That is the one he is waiting for!

7

AN URGENT MESSAGE

❖

Young Victor Maxwell loved sport. All kinds of sport. He and his mates used to kick an old rag ball or an empty Ovaltine tin up and down the street where they lived in the Donegall Road area of Belfast. And pretend they were Tommy Dickson. Or Tommy Hamill. Their big heroes.

Then Saturday came. The best day of the week, by far. Victor's dad was an Irish League referee so little son got to watch all the matches for free. Linfield in Windsor Park. Distillery in Grosvenor Park. Belfast Celtic in Celtic Park. Great!

And he loved boxing too. He and some of his friends were members of a boxing club in Lower Windsor Avenue. Indeed young Victor was knocked out more than once.

While Victor's overriding interest was in sport, others had an interest in something infinitely more important to the young lad. His soul.

Every Sunday, Victor attended the Sunday School in Richview Presbyterian Church on the Donegall Road in Belfast. There the teacher who made the most lasting impression on the young lad was Billly Hamilton. This man was genuinely interested in his young charges. He taught them the Bible stories and insisted that they commit many well-known Scripture portions to memory.

Someone else who took a great interest in the young people around Donegall Road in those days was Rev. John Girvin from the Belfast City Mission. He was forever chasing up the youngsters, encouraging them to attend all kinds of church activities.

When he was fourteen years of age Victor left school. And started to work in the Co-Op in Andersonstown. This made him feel good. When he moved from short trousers into long trousers he thought that he had changed from a boy into a man ! And when he was able to stop depending on his pocket-money and actually spend his very own wage he really felt grown up!

It was in the Co-Op that Victor met Ronnie Anderson, and he immediately recognised that there was something different about this older man. He was always witnessing. Always talking about Jesus.

After two years in the Co-op, Victor changed his job. At sixteen he went to work as a telegram boy in Belfast's Head Post Office. Now this was a REAL job! He was supplied with a B.S.A. 125 Bantam to ride about all over the city. It was great when he was sent to the Sandy Row or Donegall Road areas. Then he could wave to everybody he knew as he zoomed past. He imagined himself as Artie Bell or Geoff Duke now!

There were over seventy lads between the ages of fifteen and eighteen working in the telegram office at the G. P.O., but Victor became particularly friendly with one of them, Sam Patterson. This Sam was a Christian and he too witnesssed consistently to his friend.

One Friday in September, 1956, Sam asked Victor, "Where are you going on Sunday evening?"

"Oh I might go to the service in Richview and then go for a walk up the Malone Road as usual", was Victor's rather casual reply. The favourite pursuit of teenagers, both male and female, on summer Sunday evenings, was walking up and down the Malone Road. Talent-spotting!

"Why do you ask?" Victor enquired after a moment's pause. He was curious to know why Sam had suddenly become so interested in his Sunday evening exploits.

"I was just wondering if you would like to come with me to the Free Presbyterian Church on the Ravenhill Road, it's not far from your granny's house," Sam explained, "to hear a man called Paisley. He's really different! I'm quite sure you would enjoy him!"

Victor considered it. Since autumn was sneaking up, the evenings were becoming cooler. And it was getting dark so much earlier.

He decided to go with Sam to hear this "different" man. Called Paisley.

On Victor's first visit to Ravenhill Free Presbyterian Church he sat with his friend up on the gallery.

The first thing that impressed the newcomer was the enthusiastic singing. It reminded him of the singing of Don de Voss in the Jack Schuler Crusade in the King's Hall the previous summer. He had been touched by that singing. It had been from the heart. And so was this.

The singing though was nothing to the preaching. It was captivating. Victor had thought that Jack Schuler's preaching had been great. And it was. But this was something else!

This man had preached earnestly for forty-five minutes and it had just seemed like forty-five seconds! Victor was mesmerised. He was hearing things from the Bible that he had never heard before. And the preacher was very persuasive.

At the end of the service the speaker made an appeal.

The congregation sang softly, "Just as I am, without one plea...", and the Rev. Paisley's voice came gently but earnestly above it, "Come now to the Saviour, as our heads are bowed. He is waiting for you. Just come to Him now. Just as you are..."

A battle began to rage in the young man's heart. He was being torn two ways. The truths that he had learnt, as a child, from Billy Hamilton and John Girvin, became very real. Truths about sin. About heaven and hell. About the importance of making a choice.

Victor was 'almost persuaded'. He wanted so much to be saved. Knew in the depths of his heart that it was the right thing to do, but then there were these other thoughts that kept flooding in... What happens if you can't keep it? You are going to make a desperate fool of yourself... And what will all those telegram boys think of you at work tomorrow morning?

So he didn't respond. Put it off. And was glad to walk out into the crisp autumn evening.

Sam offered to take him home in his car. But no. He wanted to go for a walk on the Malone Road. So he did. Met up with some of his other mates. And tried to forget.

The next Sunday evening Victor went along himself to Ravenhill Free Presbyterian Church, and met Sam there. Again they sat in the gallery. And again the message from Rev. Paisley was powerful. Challenging. Compelling. Not surprisingly, the same battle raged in the young man's soul.

Again the appeal. "As our heads are bowed..."

Again the failure to respond. For all the very same reasons.

A few days later Victor heard about something that shocked him. Helped to emphasise to him the importance of getting right with God. And soon.

A young boy on the Donegall Road had hopped onto the back of a lorry. To steal a ride. Unfortunately, however, he had lost his grip, fallen off, and a car that was following ran right over him.

And he was dead. Gone. Finished. Just like that.

"If that had been me," he kept saying to himself. "If that had been me."

Victor became a regular attender at the Sunday evening service in Ravenhill Free Presbyterian Church. But he never had the courage to make a definite decision for Christ. Until Sunday, 28th October, that is.

That was crunch time. Big-decision day.

That evening Victor really wanted to come to Christ. He was deeply convicted of his sin. Knew that Christ was the only answer to his need. And he faced the same dilemma all over again. He had to make a choice. Heaven or hell. Christ or the world. Sin or salvation.

The appeal, was, as ever, very earnest. Very sincere. "As our heads are bowed, come to Christ. Just where, and as, you are ."

One part of him was struggling to rise and respond to the appeal. And come to the Saviour. The other half of him stayed firmly anchored to the seat. It felt as though he was being held down by some supernatural force of gravity.

Soon the appeal was over. And yet again he had let it pass.

Just as he was coming down the stairs from the gallery, Victor spotted a teenage girl from the Donegall Road area of the city. He had known Lily Campbell since childhood days. They had attended Linfield Intermediate School together.

When Lily spied him she came straight over. Like a bullet.

"What are you doing here, Victor?" she enquired.

"I just came to hear Mr. Paisley", was the somewhat non-commital response.

"Are you a Christian then?" was the next question.

"No, I'm not", Victor replied, almost under his breath.

"Well, would you not like to get saved?" Lily went on.

She wasn't going to give up easily. Victor wished for a split second that she would just go away and leave him alone. But she was waiting for an answer to her last question. And when Victor did reply, he was very honest.

"Yes, I would", he admitted, simply.

That was all that Lily needed to hear. She wasted no time.

"Come with me," she instructed. Commanded, almost.

Before he really realized what was happening, Victor found himself in the warm-and-welcoming, but in-a-certain-sense awesome, presence of the preacher. Mr. Paisley.

They went into a back room together. After Mr. Paisley had read some Scripture passages to the young man, explaining clearly the way of salvation, they both knelt down side by side. And as Mr. Paisley prayed, Victor Maxwell accepted Christ as his Saviour.

As they rose from their kness, Victor told the preacher that he had trusted Christ.

Mr. Paisley greeted this announcement with great joy. And with the assurance that the One who had saved him would never leave him throughout life. And that Victor would be with Him in heaven, forever.

As he stepped out into the night, a few minutes later, the full significance of the decision that he had just made, came home to the young convert.

It was a life-changing, and long-lasting, experience. For all of time. And for all of eternity. And there was also a wonderful sense of peace. Of tranquility. Of becoming a member of a new family.

This sense of having new friends in Christ, and a new direction in life was emphasised for him when one of the lads standing around asked him if he would like to join them in a "Bible study".

He went, with the others to a house in Rydalmere Street. There he found a group of more than twenty young people who had their Bibles with them. And they seemed to be so keen to discuss spiritual matters. That particular night they were talking about the Lord's return and future events. This was all totally new to Victor. He was amazed at all the stuff these people knew about the Bible. Thoughts and ideas that he had never even dreamed existed!

It was just all that wee bit confusing!

When he arrived home later that evening he told his parents that he had accepted the Lord Jesus Christ as his Saviour. He was a Christian.

Although they told him this was "good", his mother and father had their reservations about this latest announcement.

When their son had retired, happily, to bed, they nodded their heads, smiled and said to each other, knowingly, "When Victor was a child he wanted to be a train driver. Two years ago he was going to be a boxer. Last year it was a footballer. Now he is going to be a Christian. Wonder what it will be next?!"

Next morning, on his way into work, Victor's mind was in turmoil. How was he ever going to tell all the lads there about his newly-found faith? He was sure they would laugh at him. And he was a little apprehensive.

He needn't have worried though.

Sam Patterson had been in about ten minutes before him, and had broken the news.

So instead of having to break the ice himself, Victor arrived to a concert of largely good-natured taunts, such as, "Go on, Victor, sing us a chorus", or "Here comes the preacher", or "We believe you have seen the light, Victor. Tell us, hi, what's it like ?"

As the day progressed, however, and the work began, a couple of the other lads came up to Victor, alone, and at different times, to tell him how much they admired him. They too were Christians, they said, but had never had the courage to confess their faith, openly.

Victor was landed with his first challenge of counselling! On his first full day as a Christian. He promised to support these bashful believers.

Months passed, and Victor continued to witness to his faith. He returned to the Donegall Road, to tell Billy Hamilton of his conversion. He was delighted. Another name to "stroke off his prayer list" for salvation.

After moving around a number of churches, Victor decided to help with the work in the newly-established Free Presbyterian Church in Dunmurry, a village on the outskirts of Belfast.

This proved to be a wise decision on Victor's part. For a couple of reasons.

Firstly, it allowed him to nurture his zeal for evangelism. He was so keen to preach the Gospel, and there was plenty of scope for that in a growing church. And the fact that God seemed to be blessing his ministry, led him to contemplate something else. Perhaps he should consider serving God in a full time capacity. Perhaps even as a missionary.

The other blessing that came from the move to Dunmurry was that it was there that he began to be seen a lot more in the company of Audrey Smith. Although he had known Audrey for several years, it was only when they both moved to Dunmurry Free Presbyterian Church that they started to 'go out together'. Victor realized that he liked this girl. There was definitely something attractive about her. Something that appealed to him. And the amazing thing was that he discovered after a few months that she felt exactly the same way about him!

They were both dedicated Christians.

And each of them had decided, independently, that they wanted to serve God. Full-time.

So Victor went off to train. In the W.E.C. College in Glasgow.

Audrey also went off to train. In the Bible College of Wales. In Swansea.

During those years at Bible College, Victor felt God calling him to work as a missionary in Brazil. Although the call was very clear and definite, Victor tried to escape it, in his own mind. Make excuses. Erect barriers.

"Lord, can this be true?" he used to ask in prayer. "You want me to serve You on the other side of the world, and yet none of my family at home are Christians yet". Victor's family tolerated his "good living". Supported him in it, indeed. It was O.K. if you liked that sort of thing. But it just wasn't for them. They were so involved in the social aspect of sport of all kinds that they hadn't a lot of time to spare for "religion".

In April, 1963, Victor was asked to conduct an evangelical mission in Newtownbreda Baptist Church. So great was the interest in those meetings that they were extended for an extra week.

On the final Sunday night Victor preached earnestly from a text in Jeremiah chapter eight, "The harvest is past, the summer is ended, and we are not saved". (v.20)

One person responded to the message that night. And accepted Christ as his Saviour. Only one. But what a one! It was the preacher's own father. What a joy! And a few months later Victor's mother was also saved.

It seemed that God was stamping His seal of approval on His servant's ministry. And preparing him for further service.

Victor and Audrey were now convinced of two things.

They belonged together.

And they should go together to Brazil.

So, on 30th January 1965, Victor and Audrey were married. In Ravenhill Free Presbyterian Church. By Rev. Ian Paisley.

And within two months they set sail for Brazil. To serve God in South America.

During those early pioneering days, and in the later church-planting growth-monitoring days, God richly blessed the work of the couple who had devoted their lives to His service.

They had two daughters, and had the joy of seeing their two daughters come to faith in Christ.

In latter years Victor has used the wealth of his Christian experience to teach in a number of seminaries and Bible Colleges. He has held pastorates in U.S.A. and Belfast. And he has written a few books on Christian topics.

As a young man, starting out in work, Victor rode his telegram bike all over Belfast. Bringing people urgent messages. Then God saved him, and called him to bring another, single, urgent message. To the people of South America. Of U.S.A. Of Britain.

It was the message of the Gospel.

Looking back on that autumn night in 1956, Victor thanks God for all those who never gave up on presenting that urgent message to him. His Sunday School teacher. The Belfast City missioners. His friends at work. Sam Patterson. The girl who challenged him, Lily Campbell. And of course, his father in the faith. The man who was "different". Rev. Ian Paisley.

8

CHAIN SMOKER

❖

During a mission in Dunmurry Free Presbyterian Church in the late 1950's, a man waited behind after a service. He appeared to be about forty-five years of age.

When one of the church elders asked if he could help, the man replied, "I want to speak to Mr. Paisley."

Having said 'Goodnight' to most of the others, Rev. Paisley joined the man who wanted to speak to him.

"What's your problem, man?" the speaker enquired, gently.

"My problem is the smoking, sir," came the honest and immediate response. "I have been addicted to cigarettes all my life and I just can't break the habit. I spent more than a year in a Japanese prison camp at the end of the War. Even there I had to smoke. So I made myself a clay pipe and pulled a thread off my shirt or my old ragged shorts, and smoked it. A thread a day. Every day. Now I am totally hooked on cigarettes. I smoke almost two hundred a day sometimes..."

He seemed distressed. In need of relief. Deliverance. Freedom.

Rev. Paisley interrupted him. "You know smoking will not take you to hell, mister. It is your sins that are taking you to hell," he explained.

"If I thought the Lord could save me from cigarettes, I'd be saved right now," the man went on. It seemed as though he hadn't even heard what he had been told. He was so preoccupied with his problem.

The preacher wanted to steer him in the right direction. Away from himself and on to the Lord. "Salvation isn't some sort of anti-smoking remedy, like you read about in the papers," he counselled. "Like a pill or an injection the doctor or a chemist could give you. The Lord Jesus Christ died on the cross to take away your sin. And if you come to Him... if you trust in Him, He will remove your sin, and clean up your life."

The anguished man thumped the seat beside him with his fist, "Will you GUARANTEE me that I will have complete freedom from the cigarettes, if I come to Jesus?" he yelled, in frustration.

"I can guarantee you that if you truly come to Christ, confessing your sin, and accept him as your Saviour, he will make you a new person," Rev. Paisley replied. "The Bible says , 'If any man be in Christ, he is a new creature', or a new creation, if you like. And when He makes a different person out of you the chances are that you will never want to smoke again."

Suddenly, all the fight went out of the man. The aggressive attitude disappeared.

"I would like to be saved, Mr. Paisley," he said, quietly.

The two men knelt down at a seat and Rev. Paisley pointed the chain smoker to the Lord. And humbly, penitently, he trusted the Saviour.

Next day, at his work in Telephone House, all the man's workmates were puzzled. Their foreman, who had just seemed to light one cigarette off another, had stopped smoking! Overnight!

Just like that!

And what was more he introduced a new rule into his department. Anyone whom he caught smoking would be asked to put out the cigarette, or get out until it was finished!

Then the notices went up all around the place, 'NO SMOKING'. The new creation couldn't even tolerate the smell of smoke!

His old cronies were very sceptical when he informed them that he was saved. That God had made a new man of him.

"Give him a fortnight!" one of them sneered.

"Don't worry, he will be back on the 'fags' in a month!" another predicted.

It was years later, when Rev. Paisley saw the converted chain smoker at a meeting.

"How are you doing?" he enquired. "Are you not back on the cigarettes yet?!"

The man who had been so desperate for guarantees more than four years previously, laughed. "Indeed I am not!" he replied. "I hate them. I haven't smoked a single one since that night when I was saved. And you were dead right, too, Mr. Paisley. When God saved me, He changed me. Made a new person out of me. Took away my old desires. He not only gave me new life in Christ Jesus, but also complete and absolute deliverance from my addiction. Praise His Name!"

9

DO IT YOURSELF

❖

In March, 1957, Jonathan Thomas was born in India. In a little town called Karimnagar. His parents had gone to that densely-populated land as missionaries, and there they had spent many fruitful years proclaiming the good news of the Gospel.

Little Jonathan was the youngest of a family of five. He had three older sisters and a 'big brother'.

The very practical needs of their maturing family brought many concerns to the dedicated parents, so they decided, in the spring of 1960, to return to their native Canada. Although they had originally come from the prairie province of Saskatchewan, the Thomas family made their new abode in British Colombia. Near Vancouver.

After looking around for a few weeks, and making some discreet enquires, the family began attending the People's Fellowship Tabernacle in Vancouver. It was a church which seemed to have a strong evangelical emphasis in its ministry. And they liked that.

Pastor Mark Buch, who was in charge of the Fellowship Tabernacle, was 'on fire' for God. Concerned that his congregation should hear the very best speakers of the day, he invited along to his platform a series of fundamentalist preachers, amongst whom were Dr. Bob Jones (senior), and Dr. Ian Paisley.

Then came the big announcement!

In June 1967, Dr. Paisley was coming to the People's Fellowship Tabernacle to conduct a Gospel mission.

The first thing that struck young Jonathan as strange about this proposed campaign was the unusual preparation for it. Prayer. Hours of it. Jonathan's dad used to go out early in the evening and come back much, much later, having spent a long time in prayer, with others from the church. Seeking the blessing of God. And the salvation of men and women, boys and girls.

This was something new for Jonathan.

And the meetings were something else as well.

Mr. Thomas had made it abundantly clear to the three members of the family still at home that they would be expected to attend the mission on every single night. Excuses about school-work or homework would not be tolerated.

"These meetings are more important than anything you will ever hear in school", he informed them all one evening, prior to the commencement of the campaign. "Your soul's salvation is more important than anything else."

So the Thomas family began to attend every night. This was something new for them all, too. To have meetings to go to every night of the week. The most they had ever been used to was a special speaker on, at the very most, a couple of nights mid-week. To go out every night was something of a novelty, then. Something different in the life of a ten year old.

Now, on Monday night, and Tuesday night, and Wednesday night... they drove the fifteen miles from where they lived into Vancouver. To the People's Fellowship Church. To hear Dr. Ian Paisley preach.

Jonathan thought this big man was just wonderful. Here was somebody who had actually gone to prison for his principles. Yet he seemed to have plenty of time to spend with the people who came along to his mission. He shook hands with them all. Including the children. That, in particular, impressed Jonathan.

Here was a big man. A powerful man. A man of God. Who asked him his name, and then remembered it!

He even signed the fly-leaf of the young lad's Bible, and wrote a Scripture reference on it.

This man was completely different from any preacher, indeed, anybody, that Jonathan had ever met before.

The meetings generated a great interest in the city of Vancouver. A local radio talk-show host was rather antagonistic to the visit of Dr. Paisley, making a series of less-than-complimentary remarks about the 'loud-mouthed Irishman' on his programme. These observations just served to send people flocking to hear what this controversial character had to say!

By mid-week the church was crammed. People were packed into every available space, on every available chair. Those who couldn't find anywhere to sit, were happy enough to stand. Just to be there.

And Dr. Paisley preached. Faithfully. Earnestly. Each night.

He declared the P.A. system redundant. With a voice like his he didn't need a loudspeaker. He had his own. Built in.

A mighty sense of the power and presence of God was felt in those gatherings and souls were being saved. Every night, it seemed, Jonathan's dad had a story of someone else who had come to know the Saviour.

On the Friday night, which was to be the final night of the campaign, the Thomas family were seated in the gallery, as usual.

Jonathan hadn't told anybody, but he would love to be saved.

Dr. Paisley chose as his text that night 1 Peter 2 v 24. The whole building seemed to resound with the words, as he read aloud, "Who his own self bare our sins in his own body on the tree, that we, being dead to sins, should live unto righteousness: by whose stripes ye were healed."

As Dr. Paisley spoke earnestly and reverently about the passion of Christ, the headings from the sermon became embedded in young Jonathan's brain. And his soul. He sat transfixed as the big man on the platform in front of him told of, His Body, His Burden, His Bruising, His Blessing and His Bounty.

Whole phrases of that message went straight to the heart of that ten-year-old.

"Our Saviour didn't just take a body for time", the speaker explained. "It was for eternity. In glory He bears the marks of Calvary."

That was a memorable message. Preached on a memorable night.

After the sermon, Dr. Paisley made an appeal. "The Lord is dealing with souls here tonight", he declared, softly. He knew. He felt it. "If you would like to be saved just make your way quietly up to the front, and we will have a word with you. Although we can't save you, we can point you to the only one who can, the Lord Jesus Christ..."

It was certainly true that the Lord was dealing with at least one soul in the meeting that night . For He was dealing with young Jonathan Thomas. A struggle was taking place in the boy's mind. "Should I go forward? Or should I not? Am I not too young to be saved? Should I not just wait a while?"

All of a sudden he decided. He wanted to be saved. And he was going to be saved...

Turning, he whispered to his father, who was sitting beside him, "I am going down to the front."

He rose. Determined. And set off.

It seemed a long, long way, down from the gallery. Then through the main part of the church. And right up to the front.

Propelled by a sincere desire to be right with God for eternity, Jonathan made it. He stood quietly, with others, at the front of the hushed congregation. The whole atmosphere was charged with the awesome presence of God.

Glancing across to see who was beside him, Jonathan was thrilled to discover that it was one of his own sisters! She had come down too!

Later, in a small back room, Dr. Paisley talked to Jonathan, and the others, explaining, yet again, the way of salvation. When he had finished speaking to them, the preacher prayed, inviting them to come, simply and individually, to Christ.

And Jonathan did just that. He trusted the Saviour. With child-like faith.

What worried him a bit then was that he didn't experience any great sensation of excitement or exuberance, straight away. Although he told the preacher that he had trusted Christ, and was saved, he didn't feel right. He kept asking himself, 'Am I really saved or not?' His basic problem was that it had all been so simple to trust in the Lord.

'Should there not have been more to it than that?' he wondered.

As the now-saved but still-uncertain boy left the counselling room that evening, Dr. Paisley laid his hand on his shoulder, and promised, "I will keep praying for you, young lad."

That, in itself, was comforting. Could only be good.

On the way home in the car, Jonathan experienced a strange assortment of feelings. Although everyone, but everyone, seemed to be rejoicing that he had been saved, he didn't feel complete, somehow. He felt that there was something missing, but he wasn't quite sure what.

What he was experiencing was happiness without fullness. Sweetness and stillness without sparkle. Like flat lemonade.

When he arrived home, Jonathan made straight for his bedroom. There he wrestled with his problem. He prayed, in frustration. "Lord, I want to know am I saved, or not?" he enquired, earnestly.

During that period of thoughtful meditation God revealed to His newest child the reality of his conversion. As Jonathan recalled a series of Bible verses that he had learnt, he came to realize that salvation was, in essence, a very simple thing, provided at an inestimable cost. Jesus had given His life for Jonathan's sins, and all he had to do was to come, and trust Him. He had come, he had tusted in Christ, and he was assured from one of the verses that he remembered that Jesus had promised, "...him that cometh to me, I will not cast out."(John 6 v 37)

It was true enough. He was saved all right.

And he began to enjoy the assurance of salvation.

However, as the boy grew into teenage, he became attracted by the glitter of the world around him. What he really wanted was the best of both worlds. He wanted to go along to church every Sunday with his parents, and 'act saved'. As long as he said the right things and did the right things nobody at church would bother him too much.

When he was seventeen he wrote to Dr. Paisley, telling him of his salvation on that memorable night, seven years previously.

In due course he was pleased to receive a reply from the busy speaker, encouraging him and pledging his continued prayer support.

Heartwarming as this was at the time, it didn't stop Jonathan from gradually sliding more and more into the things of the world. He became almost two different people. On Sundays he did all the accepted church-type things. But on weekdays, he wanted to be just the same as all his friends at school. One of 'the lads'.

Jonathan was scared to stand up for Jesus.

He didn't want to be seen as some sort of an odd-bod. A religious crank.

And so he carried on. Trying to enjoy himself. Living a double life.

Then, in 1976, Jonathan married Arlene.

His new bride was a match for the now-working young man in a number of ways. One of them was the fact that she was, like her new husband, a Christian. And just like her new husband also, she was a feeble, fruitless one.

They were both on the way to heaven.

They were both on the way to heaven, together.

But they weren't really going anywhere else for God, fast.

One night God dealt with Jonathan.

He lay wide awake. Just couldn't get to sleep. Verses from the Bible flooded into his mind. And with them all came the clear message that he was wasting precious days. Months. Years.

He would have to do something about it. Somehow. The first step he knew that he must take, though, was to tell his wife about this overwhelming conviction that he had experienced.

How will she react? he wondered.

When the opportunity arose, a few days later, Jonathan told Arlene, in words that he had rehearsed over and over in his mind, about his sleepless night, and his desire to be effective, in some way, for God.

He needn't have worried about her reaction!

"I have been thinking that about myself for months now, Jonathan," she replied, "but I just didn't know how to put it to you."!

From that time onwards, the young couple dedicated themselves to the service of God. They determined to do something worthwhile for Him.

But where? And how?

When first married they had lived in a small town in central British Colombia but then they moved to the city of Prince George where Jonathan had been appointed as manager in an automotive repair shop.

Jonathan and Arlene began to attend the Brethren chapel in the city. There they soon became actively involved in Sunday School and Children's work and enjoyed many happy times of fellowship with the believers.

However, they were concerned at the lack of evangelical outreach from the chapel. And what disturbed them even more was that there seemed to be a lack of interest in rejuvenating any sense of evangelical witness in the church. No outside speakers were ever invited. No Gospel missions of any sort were conducted. Or even contemplated.

By the mid 1980's Jonathan and Arlene had a growing family to care for. And a growing conviction to cope with. They were both convinced that they should be more deeply involved in the work of God.

They felt that they should try to establish a local radio ministry.

Having prayed about the matter together, and discussed all the implications and possibilities of it, at length, they approached a well-known American preacher, in charge of a large fundamental ministry. They expressed their desire and burden to his organisation, assuring each prospective speaker that if he would just be willing to go on the air, and present the Gospel, they would take care of all the financial arrangements.

And in each and every single case they drew a blank.

This was frustrating, for they were sure that this was the direction in which God wanted them to go. But what could they do ?

One morning, Jonathan went down to talk to the manager of the local Radio Station about the proposed programme. The manager was sympathetic to the idea, and agreed terms for a thirty-minute Sunday-morning slot. He couldn't understand all the fuss Jonathan was making about his difficulty in finding a suitable speaker, however.

"Why don't you do it yourself ?" he asked, with genuine sincerity.

On arriving home, Jonathan tried to pass the matter off as a huge joke to his wife. "Do you know what he said to me?" he laughed. "Do you know what the man actually said? He said, 'Why don't you do it yourself?'!"

Arlene wasn't amused.

She sat quietly for a minute or two.

This suggestion that her husband seemed to find so funny was something that she had considered as a real possibility. After all, he was the one who was most enthusiastic about the idea, and he was progressing by leaps and bounds, spiritually.

"Well why DON'T you do it yourself?" she countered. "Why shouldn't you?"

She had a valid point. And so had the man in the Radio Station.

They both recognised in Jonathan what he didn't see in himself. A zeal and an ability to serve God wholly. And to present His Word both earnestly and acceptably on the radio.

So it was that in March, 1987, the first 'Search the Scriptures' Bible Study programme, led by a somewhat apprehensive, but nonetheless fulfilled, Jonathan Thomas, was broadcast.

At last God had made it possible for Arlene and he to see their vision become a reality. The Gospel was going out on the five radio stations on the local network.

And how good their God proved to be, too. Although never making any appeal for funds, their financial needs were always met. All the bills for any one month were paid in that month. People who had enjoyed the programme wrote in with words of encouragement and tokens of practical support.

During this time, their former Pastor, Mark Buch, contacted Jonathan and enquired if he would consider moving down to

Vancouver to take charge of the ministry in the People's Fellowship Tabernacle when he retired. Jonathan and Arlene took this as further confirmation that God was calling them into full-time service for Him.

Although they gave the possibility of a move to Vancouver careful and prayerful consideration, they decided independently, and then together, that this was not for them.

God seemed to be channelling their thoughts towards a totally different sphere of service.

As their burden for the radio ministry continued, Jonathan and Arlene left the Brethren chapel, in 1990, and rented a hall in another part of the city. They wanted to establish an independent work for God.

Their first morning service was small, with only nine people attending. But with great faith and much prayer they continued their work, and God continued to bless. Through radio and local contacts, others began to come. Slowly, but surely the numbers increased.

Since the hall was used as a club every Saturday night, some of the members had to attend extra-early on Sunday mornings. To brush up the cigarette ends and liquor cans, and arrange the seating for the service. The three Thomas children, Edward, Charlene and Christopher were by then old enough to play their part in this weekly clean-up.

During the early years of the 1990's the church continued to expand. Souls were saved, and Christians joined them from other places.

In 1994, Jonathan felt led of God to enter Bible College and train for full-time Christian ministry. This he did. He made application and was accepted for training in the Free Presbyterian College in Toronto.

It was when just completing his studies there that he met Dr. Paisley again. This time, however, Jonathan was doing the preaching, addressing the Presbytery of the Free Presbyterian Church of North America, and Dr. Paisley was sitting behind him on the platform. Listening.

In 1995 the steadily expanding church applied to the Free Presbyterian Church for recognition. Two ministers from that Church, Rev. Goligher from Cloverdale and Rev. Fletcher from Calgary, had been very supportive of them in the earlier, struggling days. And it was to the Free Presbyterian Church that they were most drawn.

They were pleased then, in 1995, when they were granted recognition as a church. There was only one snag, though. As yet, they had no permanent building. And they had no intention of spending the rest of their church lives brushing out a smoky club hall every Sunday morning!

In this matter, as in all the others, God was one step ahead of them.

In October, 1995, a disused church building came on the market. The United Church of Canada had closed down some months before, and their building was up for sale.

Though small in numbers, the newly-established church were convinvced that God had it just for them. So they prayed. And submitted an offer.

Then they prayed again, and again, and again...

To their great delight their offer was accepted.

God had stamped His seal of approval on their efforts for Him. Their burning desire and deep longing was that many souls would find Christ as Saviour in that new building.

So when the members of the newly-named Heritage Free Presbyterian Church moved into their new building in June, 1996, they began with an evening of prayer. There and then they thanked God for His goodness to them, and beseeched Him to honour His work in their new surroundings.

God has heard, and answered those prayers, already.

Souls have been saved, and Christians strengthened and blessed.

The Thomas children love their new church, too. Edward expressed all of their feelings one day when he said, "Going to Church is wonderful now. At least we don't have to haul equipment about and brush the place out every Sunday morning!"

In October 1997, Dr. Paisley visited Prince George, that rapidly developing city, right at the geographical heart of British Colombia.

Although Prince George is a pleasantly warm and beautiful place in summer, and a bitterly cold and beautiful place in winter, he didn't go there for a holiday.

And although the countryside beyond the city boundary teems with wildlife, he didn't go to study the bears or the moose.

Dr. Paisley had taken the time to make the long journey to that idyllic location, far to the west of the Rockies, for one purpose. And for one purpose only.

It was to speak at the ordination of Jonathan Thomas as a minister of the Free Presbyterian Church. What a wonderful thrill that day was for Jonathan. As he sat listening to the big man whom he so much admired, the man whom he respected as a spiritual giant, though now thirty years older, speak with the same zeal and fervour as he had done on the night when he had heard him speak, and had come to Christ, he praised God for that night. And for His leading and guiding in his life in the thirty years that lay between.

"How good is the God we adore", he thought.

Over and over again.

10

IMPERSONATION!

❖

Saturday night had just given way to Sunday morning and Ian and Eileen Paisley were preparing to retire for the night, when the doorbell rang in their Beersbridge Road home.

It was12.40 a.m.. Twenty to one.

"Be careful who you open the door to at this time of night, Ian," Mrs. Paisley warned, as her husband made for the door.

"Don't you worry about me, Eileen. It will be all right," he replied. "You just go on to bed."

When Dr. Paisley opened the door, there stood a well-dressed gentleman. Expensive overcoat and hat. Black rolled umbrella. Looked like money.

"Can I come in ?" the stranger asked.

"Yes, come ahead," Dr. Paisley invited, completely ignoring his wife's warning of two minutes before. He sensed this man posed no threat. He was in some kind of need.

He was right. As the man stepped into the porch he started to sob, like a child.

"Man, are you in some sort of trouble?" Dr. Paisley enquired, feeling really sorry for him. He looked so dejected.

"I'm in trouble all right," came the reponse. "And I hope you don't mind me calling at this time of night, but I just had to tell you about it."

Recognising that this stranger had a genuine concern of some kind that needed to be addressed, the man of the house ushered him into the sitting-room. When the light was switched on, he saw that his nocturnal visitor was weeping uncontrollably. Big tears just rolled down his cheeks.

"Mr. Paisley, I want you to forgive me," he cried out in anguish. "Please, forgive me."

Ian Paisley was puzzled. So puzzled that he chuckled, quietly. "Forgive you. Forgive you..." he repeated. "Forgive you for WHAT? I don't even know you, man. So how could I forgive you? Who are you anyway?"

The visitor pulled his wallet from an inside pocket. Opening it, he produced a card which he handed to his mystified host.

This agitated man was a director in a leading Belfast company.

Replacing his card in the wallet, he burst out again. "You will understand when I tell you my story. You see I have mocked you! Oh how I have mocked you! Please will you forgive me?"

"How have you mocked me? I still don't understand what you are talking about," Dr. Paisley went on.

They both sat down, and the man began to tell his 'story'.

"Well, it is like this," he explained. "I run a prosperous business here in the city. But I am also a mimic. An impersonator, call it what you will. I go around clubs and concerts and society socials in the evenings doing impressions of people. Mocking them, really. I entertain large audiences.

One day some of the lads that work for me suggested, "You know, you ought to go round to the Ulster Hall some Sunday night, boss, and hear Paisley preaching. Then you could do a turn for us on a Monday morning."

Good idea, I thought. So I did it. I went to the Ulster Hall to hear you. I noted all the gestures that you used when you were preaching. All the intonations of your voice. And what it was that you said.

Then I went in and did a show for the boys at the tea-break on Monday morning. I mocked you. And they loved it. They yelled and roared and laughed and cheered me to the echo.

When they were leaving to go back to whatever part of the firm it was that they worked in, I told them, "I will go back to the Ulster Hall next Sunday night, boys. Our next show will be next Monday morning!"

So I went the next Sunday night, but it was different, Mr. Paisley. You preached a sermon that night that knocked the nonsense out of me! I ended up not watching you to mimic you. I was listening to every word that you said. And it was hitting me hard, right in the heart.

Next morning the boys were all crammed into every available nook and cranny in my office when I arrived for work. They couldn't even wait to the tea-break to see me impersonate you. They wanted the show there and then. "What about the turn on Paisley, boss?" some of them asked, expectantly.

I just couldn't do it, Mr. Paisley. So I turned on them. "Get out of my office every single one of you!" I roared. "I don't want to talk about that man any more! I don't even want to think about him any more!" The boys gave me funny looks, then trooped out in silence. They couldn't understand what had come over me. In fact, I'm not very sure that I understand it myself..."

He paused. Just to make sure that Dr. Paisley was still listening. He was, intently. So the story continued...

"That was six weeks ago and I haven't had one minute's peace since. I have been in agony. Absolute agony, all this time."

Then, lowering his voice, he made the enquiry that had brought him there. "Mr. Paisley, is there any hope for me? I have made a fool of Jesus and the man who preached him. I have made jokes about the blood, and heaven, and hell, and sin, and mercy, and God... Do you think that God would still forgive me, and save me?"

When he was sure that his visitor had finished all that he had to say, the man who had been so cruelly caricatured replied, "Yes, He can. And He will. The Bible says that He 'is not willing that any should perish'.

The concerned man's countenance cleared considerably.

"Say that again," he urged.

"God is not willing that any should perish," Dr. Paisley repeated. Then he added the second half of the verse , "...But that all should come to repentance."

"'Any' and 'all', that takes you in, doesn't it?" he went on to ask.

"It does indeed," the seeking soul was excited to discover. "Can I be saved, now?"

"Yes, you can. You most certainly can!" Dr. Paisley assured him.

They knelt down together at the settee in the sitting-room. Side by side. The mimic and the mimiced. And the one who had been mocked led the one who had mocked him to saving faith in the One who had been mercilessly mocked by wicked men, before dying for the both of them, Jesus Christ.

There then followed a 'Hallelujah' prayer meeting, second to none. Enough to waken the neighbourhood at two o'clock in the morning, not to mention the house!

Dr. Paisley praised God that He had brought another soul to Himself. Another 'son unto glory.'

And the man who had come to the Paisley home in tears, continued in tears. But the tears were of a different variety. They were tears of unbelievable happiness.

The Saviour he had joked about had given him joy.

The God he had mocked had forgiven him. And given him peace. Marvellous!

No wonder he couldn't stop crying!

11

HEAVEN'S BARRICADES ON HELL'S BROAD ROAD

❖

John Mc Dowell and Roy Gillespie had much in common. They were both staunch loyalists and office-bearers in the Orange Order and the Royal Black Preceptory.

They each had wives called Ruby.

Though neither man was saved, they both attended Gospel services regularly. They went to these meetings on a Sunday night, sometimes to the Free Presbyterian Church in Ballymena, and sometimes to the Ulster Hall in Belfast. They went there, not because they were in any way interested in the Gospel. For they weren't. Meetings and church might be O.K. for little old ladies in felt hats and fur boots, they reckoned, but it wasn't for them. They had more important things to attend to.

Anyway, they considered themselves to be every bit as good as all these church-going types.

They went along to church and meetings to hear a political leader whom they very much admired, speaking. That man was Rev. Ian Paisley. They supported the political stance of his Protestant Unionist

Party, and followed him to parades and rallies all over the Province.

As they came to know the forthright preacher and politician better, both Roy and John realized that he had another side to his character far removed from the hard-line political activist as he was often portrayed.

It was a deeply spiritual side. A genuinely caring side. A side that was more interested in their soul than their sash.

Nearly every time they talked, either face-to-face or on the phone, Rev. Paisley told them that he was praying for them. That they would be saved.

If John or Roy made any response at all to these "religious remarks", as they saw them, it was always very non-committal. Low key. They had no intention whatsoever of being saved.

Yet they hardly ever missed a Sunday night at the Ulster Hall. Just in case the preacher would give an update on the political situation, and they would miss it...

Then came the big challenge for both of them.

At the beginning of September, 1975, Rev. Ian Paisley commenced a Gospel mission in Ballymena Town Hall. No politics here. Just straight Gospel preaching.

Both Roy and John had told their wives that they had no intention of going to that. Ever, at all.

They hadn't reckoned on the power of prayer, however. Before the mission began, and as it got under way, many Christians around Ballymena started to pray earnestly for their friends and relatives. Including John and Roy.

Ruby Gillespie had a burden for the people of her district, many of whom would go to the mission in Ballymena, if only she could get them there.

What she really needed was a minibus. And a driver.

During a prayer meeting she felt guided to ask a local young Christian man, Derek Irwin, if he would be willing to drive a minibus, and pick up people from the Ahoghill and Cullybackey areas, if she could obtain the use of one.

He said he would. Here was a way in which he could further the work of the Lord.

All Ruby needed now was the minibus.

Next day she phoned a local contractor, George Boville, and told him of her burden. And her need of a minibus to tranport people into Ballymena.

"Certainly, Mrs. Gillespie," was George's reply. "You can have our minibus for the mission every night you need it. And don't you worry about fuel, either. We will make sure that it is filled with diesel for every trip".

When Ruby told her husband, Roy, about George Boville's kindness, his instant response was, "Oh, that is very good. But I hope you're not expecting me to drive it. For I won't be!"

Deep down in his heart, Roy would have loved to be able to drive that minibus. But he couldn't. Not because he wasn't competent. But because he wasn't a Christian.

He was peeved about that. It got to him. Convicted him, in a strange sort of way. There was something missing in his life.

"Don't worry, Roy," his wife retorted. "I have already a driver lined up. Derek Irwin has promised to drive it for us."

On the second Sunday of the mission, Roy decided that since his wife had been going to these meetings for a whole week, every night, and seemed to be enjoying them, he would go with her to the Sunday afternoon meeting. Just to please her. And to see what exactly was going on.

Little did he know that his change of mind, was really nothing much to do with him at all! It was an answer to so many fervent prayers. A work of the Holy Spirit.

He attended the meeting, and many were surprised, yet delighted to see him there. But it meant nothing to him. So much prayer, and praise, and preaching. And people going forward for counselling.

It all left him cold. Unmoved.

Then came that remarkable night. Tuesday, 9th September, 1975.

John's wife Ruby, who like her husband was a great admirer of Rev. Paisley, and who was, also like her husband, still unsaved, had been attending the meetings every night with some of her friends. They went into Ballymena in a minibus.

Ruby had always been telling John about the meetings. And telling him that he "should go". Up until then he had always put her off. With some paltry excuse.

At work that day, he could get no peace in his heart. Or soul. Or mind. There was always this sense of restlessness with him. He knew that he should go to the mission. And determined to go that very night. To see if he could, in some way rid himself of this burden that was pressing down on him. Spoiling his happiness...

On arriving home from work, John discovered that his wife was ready to go out to the meeting. She invited him to get ready and come with her. But he refused, making the excuse that he didn't have time. After all, as he pointed out to her, he hadn't even had his dinner yet!

As soon as she had left the house, though, John changed his mind. And his clothes.

Leaving his dinner uneaten, he set out in the car, alone. Destination, the Town Hall, Ballymena.

Roy had decided to go back with his wife again on that Tuesday night. He sat between Ruby, and his sister-in-law, Jane. The Town Hall was packed. People were flocking in. Trying to find seats.

What is bringing all these people here? he wondered to himself. There must be something supernatural drawing them.

His sense of wonder deepened, when he noticed that his fellow-Orangeman, John Mc Dowell, was sitting a few rows in front of them.

As the stewards were struggling to accommodate all the people who were still crowding in, the singing began. It was enthusiatic singing of old-fashioned Gospel hymns.

By the time the speaker stood up to announce his text, the Hall was packed full with subdued but expectant people.

The text was taken from 2 Peter chapter 3. It was verse 9. Rev. Paisley read it out, solemnly. "The Lord is not slack concerning his promise, as some men count slackness ; but is longsuffering to us-ward, not willing that any should perish, but that all should come to repentance."

The congregation, crushed together on every available seat, or standing, around the walls, heads bowed reverently, then listened with rapt attention as the preacher ennumerated 'Heaven's Barricades on Hell's Broad Road"..

The barricades of the Word of God... a mother's influence... Gospel sermons... the convicting power of the Holy Spirit... the death of Christ...

A powerful sense of the presence of God pervaded that meeting. No one stirred or moved. Everybody was listening, as though it was the last Gospel message they were ever going to hear.

Then came the appeal. The speaker knew that God was moving in the hearts of many in the audience. He felt that God was dealing directly with his faithful friends. And he referred to them as he spoke.

"There are some people here who are good friends of my own", he began. "They have supported me in political life. They are good friends of mine , but they haven't met my Saviour. What joy it would be if you should be saved tonight."

Then, addressing the whole silent congregation, he went on, "As our heads are bowed, and our eyes are closed, and the people of God are all praying, I am going to make this simple appeal. Is there a man or woman, boy or girl, who is going to accept Christ as their Saviour? Come to the Saviour tonight...?"

As the appeal continued, and two hymns were sung, there was movement in the Town Hall, Ballymena. People began to leave their seats, and move into the counselling-room, "at the front, to your right". But this steady stream of seeking souls represented more than merely a movement of people.

It signified a movement of God.

Still John Mc Dowell sat in his seat. And so too, did Roy Gillespie. A battle was raging in each man's soul. God or the world. Satan or the Saviour.

As the final hymn was announced, John made his choice. He prayed silently, "Lord, save me", and at that moment he simply placed his faith and trust in Christ.

And having made that important decision, it wasn't long until he wanted to let others know about it, too. He was prepared to 'stand up and be counted' for his new Lord and Master. While the strains of:

"I've wandered far away from God,
Now I'm coming home,
The paths of sin, too long I've trod,
Now I'm coming home..."
echoed reverently around the capacity congregation, John stood to
his feet, and marched, like a soldier on parade, to the front.

What an answer to prayer!

The speaker recognised it as such. As the singing died away, he
said quietly, "A dear man has just come there. I have prayed for that
man for a long time. If only that man came, it would all have been
worthwhile..."

And as John entered the counselling-room, Rev. Jim Beggs
announced, in the glow of the triumph of answered prayer, "Make
room for that man!"

Unknown to John at that moment, his bold action in standing to
his feet and setting off for the front, had a vital impact on his friend
Roy, sitting behind him.

It was like an electric shock. But it proved to be a catalyst that
helped spur him into crucial action.

Just before a 'definitely-must-be-the-last' singing of, 'I've
wandered far away from God', Rev. Paisley, visibly moved by the
events taking place around him, made the final final appeal.

And Roy saw it as just for him.

"Friend, I know you and I love you", he pleaded, with obviously
genuine warmth. I would do anything to get you to the cross. But I
can't carry you. If I could, I would. If I could have carried you to
Calvary, you would have been saved long ago..."

The two women on either side of Roy were both sitting, heads
bowed, praying passionately for him. Roy sat, with his feet up on the
chair in front. The war being waged in his soul had come to the last,
decisive battle.

Words that he had heard in some meeting, somewhere in the past,
flashed into his mind, "My Spirit shall not always strive with man..."
Could this possibly be his last chance?

John Mc Dowell was at the front. He had gone for it...

Suddenly, the Lord spoke to him. Very directly. "It's now or never", He said. At that moment Roy also trusted in the Lord for salvation. He came to the place called Calvary. Himself. Drawn by the love of the dying Saviour and transported on the wings of thousands of prayers. And there he saw that Jesus had died on that cross for him, just as if there hadn't been another single person in the world.

Then, to the delight of all the praying Christians in the Town Hall, he also rose, walked up, and into the counselling-room. What he saw in there made a lasting impression on him.

There were far more people jammed into that little room than it was ever designed to accommodate. John was there, rejoicing in his salvation. And there seemed to be dozens more. Men, women and young people. Many of them weeping openly, wanting to be saved. Busy counsellors with open Bibles were busy counselling seeking souls. A number were on their knees...

God was at work. In a mighty way.

When the meeting was over, Rev. Paisley went into the counselling-room. He read the Scriptures and prayed with Roy. Whatever it was that he said meant nothing to the new convert, however. For although he was saved, another battle had begun within his soul.

Satan hadn't given up on him. Yet.

He began to bombard Roy's mind from another angle, now.

"Haven't you made a right fool of yourself in front of all those people?" he suggested. "What if you aren't saved at all? They are going to have a great laugh at you, are they not...?"

Roy left the room, saved, but afflicted by doubts.

On his way out of the Town Hall, he met John Mc Auley, a prominent Christian from the town.

When John told him that he was 'glad to hear the good news', Roy, still in mental and spiritual anguish, made a simple request.

"John, please pray for me. That I might know that I'm saved," he begged.

Aware of the struggle taking place in Roy's soul, John complied with that request. Immediately. There and then, standing at the top of the stairs, he prayed with, and for, the beleaguered new believer.

When he eventually made it out on to the street, to take the bus home, Roy saw his friend, John Mc Dowell. And John was radiant. Beaming all over. Rejoicing in the joy of his salvation. A grown man, but a babe in Christ.

He just looked, so very, very happy.

Roy didn't feel that way at all. He felt as though there was a ten-ton weight pressing down on the top of his head. And he kept thinking, "Surely you couldn't be saved. Look at all these Christians. They all appear so happy. And you just feel so miserable."

When he had taken his seat in the bus, and just before it set off on its packed-with-mostly-happy-people homeward country run, Roy began to sing. Spontaneously.

They were well known words. Words that he had sung so often. In church services. At weddings. And funerals.

"The Lord's my shepherd, I'll not want,
He makes me down to lie,
In pastures green, He leadeth me
The quiet waters by."

All those within earshot stopped their chatter. To hear Roy sing. They thought that he must be so content. So much at peace.

Really, the opposite was true. He was seeking for consolation. Assurance. Lasting inner peace.

Not long after he and Ruby had arrived home, the phone started to ring.

It was different people, concerned people, genuine Christian people, to tell him that his conversion was a wonderful answer to their prayers.

Roy tried ever so hard to sound enthusiastic. Without ever feeling it.

Then he picked up a Bible. He would turn to the Word of God. Surely there must be a verse, or a passage, in it that could reassure him...

Opening it at Psalm 23, he began to read the words that he had sung in the bus.

"The Lord is my shepherd," he read aloud.

Ruby, who was standing beside him, remarked quietly, "That's right, Roy. The Lord is your Shepherd."

"The Lord is MY shepherd," he thought.

Slowly, surely, a soothing sense of security enveloped his struggling soul.

It was the Lord, not Rev. Ian Paisley, who was his Shepherd.

And it was the Lord, not Rev. Paisley, who had saved him. Salvation was of God alone.

He was now in living, vital contact with the Lord Himself. And He could and would keep him throughout his life. Indeed, right into eternity, too. For he was going to dwell in the house of the Lord. Forever.

That did it. He was saved, and sure of it. Satisfied, and glad of it.

Now, he also could rejoice in the joy of his salvation.

On the very next night Roy went back to the mission in Ballymena Town Hall. Driving a bus, full of people from his neighbourhood!

God hadn't finished pouring out His blessings on the two couples after both John and Roy came to know the Lord, on that memorable Tuesday night, however. For on the Thursday night, John's wife, Ruby, was saved as well.

What joy and rejoicing! What wonderful, wonderful blessing!

More than twenty years have passed since that mission in Ballymena Town Hall, which was described by many who were present as, "As near a thing to Revival as we have ever seen".

Yet John and Roy, with their wives, and many more who were saved at those meetings, can honestly affirm that the Lord has indeed been their Shepherd, all down the years.

They have lacked nothing.

And the future, too, looks bright. Things are set to get better.

They are going to dwell in Heaven with their Lord. Forever.

12

NOT A POLITICAL MATTER

❖

After Mrs. Eileen Paisley had been elected to Belfast City Council she was sitting one day in her Advice Centre in Sandy Row.

When a well-dresssed middle-aged man came in she was prepared to hear what he had to say. To assist and advise him however possible.

The man began with an apology. "I am not from this area," he said, "but I feel I need to talk to somebody like yourself."

"Don't worry about that," Mrs. Paisley assured him. "If I can help you in any way, I will."

"My problem is," the newcomer soon revealed, "that I have been seeking salvation for a long time. I know I need to be saved. And I want to be saved. Can you tell me how?"

It gave Mrs. Paisley tremendous joy to lay aside the hum-drum, run-of-the-mill, grants-and-gripes business of her Advice Centre and point that seeking soul to the Saviour.

On the way out, the newly-saved and much-happier man thanked Mrs. Paisley for her 'time'.

"My job is to help the people of Belfast in whatever way I can," she told him. "And by far the most important way that I can help them in time, is to make sure that they are prepared to meet God in eternity. It was only a privilege."

Shortly after Dr. Paisley was first elected as M.P. for North Antrim he began conducting a series of Advice Centres around the area. This afforded him the opportunity to meet the people in the rural areas, and to discuss farming subsidies, housing benefits and a whole wider range of topics with them.

Mid-afternoon on one such day, two women in their twenties came into the Bushmills Centre.

Sometimes Dr. Paisley could guess what people wanted when they came into the Centres. They produced official-looking brown envelopes from pockets, handbags, or well-thumbed folders. That meant "Help!" These women had nothing with them, though. They were giving nothing away. He would have to ask.

"Well, ladies, how can I help you?" he enquired.

The woman who appeared perhaps slightly older, spoke. "We hope you don't mind," she said, "but this is not a political matter. It's just that my friend and I here would like to be saved. And we thought that you would help us if we came to see you."

"Indeed I will. And only too happy to do so," their M.P. replied, warmly. This was the kind of problem he liked to solve for people.

Having made a half-neat pile of all the constituency clutter on his desk, he placed his Bible on top of it. After leafing through it for a few moments he found a number of appropriate verses of Scripture. These he read to the ladies, explaining from them God's way of salvation.

Then, individually, each of those women accepted Christ as Saviour. Sitting there in the office.

Dr. Paisley prayed with them, and they left, content.

Their problem which had not been political, but spiritual, had been brought to a soul-satisfying and eternal conclusion.

On a Thursday afternoon in the late 1980's, the phone rang in Dr. Paisley's European office, in Belfast. Mrs. Paisley was in attendance.

"Hello. How may I help you?" she enquired of the caller.

"I would like an appointment with Dr. Paisley. And it's urgent," a man's voice answered. He was obviously in some sort of desperation.

"I'm sorry Dr. Paisley is out of the country at the present," Eileen informed him, "but I am his wife. Could I be of any assistance?"

The caller sounded relieved when he replied, "I'll talk to anybody as long as I can get some satisfactory answers. But it will take me half-an-hour to make it to your place. I am up in the country here, near Dromara."

"Don't worry about that," Mrs Paisley assured him. "I will be here for a while yet. I will wait for you."

When the man arrived in the office, forty minutes later, he had his wife, his mother-in-law and his three children with him! A whole car-load!

After she had ushered them all into her husband's office, the most private room in the building, Mrs. Paisley found chairs for everybody.

The man began to explain their reason for coming, by saying, "I hope you don't mind us coming here like this, especially as ours is not a political problem. It's a long story, though, so I couldn't tell you it all over the phone."

Mrs. Paisley settled herself in her chair, and regarded the anxious family across the desk. "I am in no hurry. Take your time and tell me all about it," she told him.

Then the whole story came out.

"I was brought up a Roman Catholic," the man began, "but I stopped going when I was seventeen or eighteen. Then I met my wife here and she was a Protestant. We were married in her church and started to go there.

Although we have a very happy marriage, and my wife is a great manager and great with the children, I have no peace in my heart. I know there is something wrong. Something missing. I have talked to our minister about this a number of times and he told me not to worry. "You will be O.K. as long as you do the best you can," he said. I have started to go to church nearly every Sunday to hear him preaching, but I'm still not satisfied."

The speaker paused and looked around. All eyes were upon him, and as everybody seemed to be waiting for more, he went on, "Last week I heard a tape of Rev. William Mc Crea singing and I thought that what he was singing about was what I want. I saw a poster somewhere advertising a meeting he is singing at in Ballynahinch next Sunday night. I was planning to go to that and then it dawned on me that if I could somehow get to Ian Paisley something might happen. So here I am."

Although he thought he had finished, he suddenly remembered that he hadn't come alone.

"Here we all are," he concluded, trying to smile.

Mrs. Paisley recognised the man's need straightaway.

He needed to be saved. He was a genuinely seeking soul.

"You know you don't need to wait until Sunday night for something to happen," she said to them all, though addressing the spokesman. "You can be saved now. You can find peace and joy and satisfaction sitting here in this office."

His eyes opened wide in a curious mixture of realization and consternation. "Really?" he replied. "That's what I have been searching for through all these years!"

Mrs. Paisley then explained to them all simply how they could be saved through faith in Jesus Christ. And the man bowed his head and trusted in Him almost at once.

Then his wife said, "I would like to be saved, too."
And Mrs. Paisley pointed her to the Lord.

The mother-in-law, who had been a silent childminding witness to all the goings-on, then remarked, "I have never heard the like of that before. I would like to get saved, too."

And Mrs. Paisley pointed her to the Lord.

All three of them were saved within the space of half-an-hour and left the office rejoicing in new life in Christ.

Household salvation! Definitely not a political matter!

13

A CUPFUL OF SIN

❖

It was a beautiful summer Sunday afternoon in 1956. Young Noel Stevenson's mother had said 'Cheerio' to her twelve year old son at the door of their Woodstock Road home, in east Belfast. Noel was on his way out to Sunday School in the Ravenhill Road Free Presbyterian Chuch.

Or so she thought.

However, Noel and a few of his companions had other ideas. When they met up on their way round to the Church they decided that it was 'far too nice a day to sit in Sunday School for an hour'.

So they 'mitched'. Played truant.

Spent the time lying about, and wandering about, nervously, in the Ormeau Park. Watching all the others who were lying about, and wandering about, contentedly, in the Ormeau Park.

When Noel arrived home about the normal time, his mother started quizzing him about the Sunday School. He should have known it would happen. For it nearly always did. Who did he see? .. Who did he walk home with?.. What was the lesson about?.. It seemed to go on and on.

When mother discovered that her young son wasn't able to give convincing answers to her questions, she suddenly asked, "Were you even there at all?"

The speed and depth of her perception caught Noel unawares. He hung his head, sheepishly. "No, I wasn't," he confessed. "Me and my mates thought it was too nice a day to sit in Sunday School so we..."

Mother didn't wait to hear any more. She was listening to no excuses. She was on her way into the kitchen for the shoebrush. And when she came back she used it. Whacked him with it!

Noel's parents were both Christians and they tried to bring their family up 'in the fear and admonition of the Lord'. So they sent them along to the Friday night Children's Meeting in the Ravenhill Road Free Presbyterian Church, and to the afternoon Sunday School. And there Noel Stevenson, as a child, heard the Gospel faithfully taught and preached.

When he turned fourteen, though, he decided that he was 'too big' for Sunday School. So he left. Although he didn't attend Sunday School any more, Noel didn't stop going to Church completely. For a while at least. He used to go along to the Sunday evening service now and again.

He liked the preacher. Rev. Paisley's robust, no-holds-barred, sock-it-to-them approach to preaching appealed to him. It was the man, and not the message, that attracted the teenage lad.

At fifteen, Noel left school and found a job. Now that he had some money in his pocket he also found that there were any number of godless companions who would show him how to spend it.

Weeks were for work. Weekends were for pleasure.

On Saturday mornings, Noel played football in a minor league competition. Then the remainder of the day was spent gambling, drinking, dancing. With no thought whatsoever about God. Or salvation. Or eternity. All that mattered was 'having a good time'.

Noel tried to hide his new style of life from his parents. He loved and respected them. And he didn't want to hurt them. There was no doubt that if they ever discovered what he was 'up to' they would be very disappointed. Shocked, even.

He used to try and avoid the creaks on the stairs when he came in during the early hours of a Sunday morning. He dreaded, above anything, wakening them. For they would catch him on...

It was inevitable, though, that they would find out, sooner or later. And they did. Noel's mother couldn't help but notice the smell of liquor on his breath. So she asked him about it. And confession time had come around again for her son. He told her , 'Yes.' She was right. He did take 'the odd drink'.

Noel's predictions of how such news would affect her had been spot on. She was both shocked and disappointed. And her reaction showed both emotions. There was suppressed annoyance. And silent tears.

As a Christian mother, however, she had her own secret weapon to use in each and every situation. It was called prayer.

There was something that always pierced and burned into the heart of the young man, like a flaming arrow, when he was going out, all dressed up, for his Saturday night 'fling'. As he came down the stairs he opened the living-room door on the way past, to speak in to his parents. Tell them he was 'away'. His mother would have been sitting in her armchair, knitting. Her cheeks would be flushed by the glow of the fire, and her lips would be moving. Noel knew fine well that she wasn't counting stitches, though. She was praying for him. Praying for her wayward son, who was breaking her heart. That God would protect him, preserve him, but above all, save him...

And even before she prayed, God was preparing His answer.

On Sunday evening, 4th November, 1962, Noel attended the service in Ravenhill Free Presbyterian Church. The speaker was an Indian pastor called Gordon Khan. As this was Pastor Khan's first visit to Northern Ireland, the meeting had been widely advertised and Noel went along out of curiosity.

On his way out of the meeting, Bertie Weir, a man from the church who knew and recognised Noel, invited him back into the Young People's Service that was to follow.

It was in there that Noel Stevenson was convicted of his sin. Not by anything that a preacher said, but by that group of young people themselves, most of whom seemed to be around his own age. They all seemed to be so happy. So full of the joy of the Lord. Exuberant. The light on their faces as they launched into one chorus after another challenged Noel.

He sat quietly in his seat looking around. And listening. Then he said to himself, "Here's me, out on the booze last night. Trying to make myself happy. Yet these people are really happy. What they have is what I need."

As the young people of the group were dispersing later, Noel approached one of the leaders whom he knew as Billy Balmer.

"I would like to speak to Rev. Paisley sometime, Billy," he said.

"O.K." Billy replied. "We can arrange that, no problem. He is away preaching up the country somewhere tonight, but I will take you up to the manse and we can wait for him there."

So Billy Balmer and Noel Stevenson walked through the streets of east Belfast that November evening. Up to the manse on the Beersbridge Road.

It was almost eleven o'clock when the busy preacher arrived home. And Noel was patiently waiting for him. He knew what he wanted. It was peace and satisfaction in his soul. The kind of peace and satisfaction that he had seen on display earlier in the evening.

As the others were all in the living-room, Rev. Paisley and Noel retired to the kitchen, and sat down at the table. They had business to do with God.

In order to illustrate the way of salvation, as simply as he could, to the convicted sixteen-and-a-half year old, the wise soul-winner placed two cups in front of them. And there they sat. Two lonely cups in the middle of a large table.

Lifting one cup with his right hand, he said, "Now look, Noel. This cup here is full of your sin." Then slowly, but deliberately he moved that cup over and allowed it to glide down inside the one that remained, alone, in the centre of the table.

"The Lord Jesus took your sins at Calvary. God placed them upon Him. Just the way I placed one cup inside the other there," he explained.

Noel understood the illustration at once. But he was afraid that he wasn't ready to be saved, somehow. Thought that he should have felt more distressed. More worked up about the whole thing.

"Mr. Paisley, I don't feel like crying," he admitted, honestly.

The preacher smiled faintly. He had dealt with all kinds of situations and degrees of emotion before. His response to the young man's concern about his lack of an outward show of feelings, was a Scriptural one. "Noel, the Bible says, 'Whosoever shall call upon the name of the Lord shall be saved.' It's not, 'Whosoever feels like crying,'" he replied.

At that point, Noel stood up. He didn't know just what he was going to do. Perhaps he should go home. But if he was going to do that, he had a request to make.

"Mr. Paisley, will you pray for me?" he begged.

The minister was prepared to pray for Noel. He was prepared to pray for anybody. But recognising the stage the seeking soul was at, he came back with, "Do you not think it is about time you started to pray for yourself, Noel?"

"Yes, I think it is," the lad confessed.

"Why not just call upon the Lord to save you, then?" the gentle big man suggested. "We will both kneel down at our chairs and you can do that."

They knelt down and Noel looked across at his counsellor. He was a big man standing up. But kneeling down he seemed to half-fill the kitchen. "Mr. Paisley, do you know I'm bad?" he enquired. The tears were beginning to come now.

"Yes, I know you're bad, Noel," came the response. "But it was people like you, bad people, that Jesus died for."

They bowed their heads again. There was an awkward silence. A deep silence. Other household sounds began to penetrate. Noel was struggling. Trying to pray. But he had a problem.

"I don't know what to say!" he blurted out, eventually.

"Just ask the Lord to save you, Noel," Rev. Paisley encouraged. He was leading the young man to Christ, slowly but surely. Kindly and lovingly.

Suddenly the silence was broken.

Noel found his voice.

"Come into my heart... Come into my heart...Come into my heart, Lord Jesus..." he cried out in anguish. It wasn't a very fluent prayer. Or very clever... But it was sincere. Genuine. It came from the very depths of his soul.

Noel Stevenson had found more than his voice. He had found the Saviour.

Rev. Ian Paisley reached across the chairs, and shook his hand. "Praise the Lord!" he exclaimed.

As Noel and Billy set out to walk home, Billy said, "You know, Noel, you should tell your mate what has happened."

"I suppose I should," the new convert replied, not quite sure that he wanted to, just at that very minute. Recognising it as the right thing to do, though, he followed on with, "I will go round by his house now, and let him know."

After Noel had knocked the door, his friend's mother opened it. She was surprised to see Noel standing there.

It was almost midnight.

"I have called to see Robert," Noel explained.

"He has gone up to bed, but I will call him for you," the puzzled woman volunteered. Noel and her son were best mates, and they had done some crazy things together, but calling for him at ten to twelve was a new one on her!

A few minutes later Robert came down the stairs. In his pyjamas. Looking dazed and dozy. Noel didn't wait for his mate to ask, "What brings you here at this time of night?"

While Robert rubbed his eyes, he told him.

"I just came round to tell you that I have got saved tonight, Robert. So the drinking, the gambling, the dancing, the football... It all goes as from now.." he announced, boldly.

Robert stared at his friend. Astonished. Incredulous.

Last night they had drunk and danced the night away in the Fiesta Ballroom. Now here was Noel, standing in the middle of his living room in the middle of the night, telling him it was all finished!

"O.K. my old mate, O.K." he replied, flabbergasted. Words failed him. He just didn't know how to respond to a drastic 'about turn' like that.

Noel left. And headed for home.

When he tiptoed up the stairs, it was well after midnight. He knocked on the door of his parents' bedroom, pushed it open and went in.

"I just called to tell you that I got saved there tonight," he announced, for the second time within the space of an hour.

This time the reaction was wonderful.

Dad sat bolt upright in the bed and shouted, "Hallelujah!"

Mum jumped out of bed, ran over and hugged her son. And hugged him and hugged him.

A mother's prayers had been answered.

Noel started to attend Ravenhill Free Presbyterian Church, and there he discovered things that he never before knew existed. He had already experienced the joy of salvation. Now he discovered the joy of Christian fellowship. And the prevailing power of prayer. He had witnessed patient, persistent prayer in the life of his godly mother. At the Church he found men who were prepared to spend hours, all night, sometimes, in prayer for souls. In tears. And the prayer meetings were packed out.

There was one minor problem that clouded Noel's mind for a while after his conversion. It kept niggling away at him. He would have to get it sorted out.

It was about his new football boots. They were the very latest 'Continental' style, and he was very proud of them. Indeed, they had cost him quite a lot of his hard-earned money, just before he was saved.

He approached Rev. Paisley with his problem, one night after a prayer meeting.

"Mr. Paisley, I have been playing a wee bit of football in the Saturday morning league," he began. "And I have just bought myself a brand new pair of boots. What do you think I should do about the football?"

Although Noel had told Robert that the football was 'finished', he had a hankering to go back. Not because he had any great love for the game, but because he wanted to get his money's worth out of his boots.

Rev. Paisley was wise. "Would you feel happy taking the Lord Jesus with you into the dressing-room and onto the pitch, where His name is so often blasphemed, Noel?" he enquired, gently.

He hadn't said, "No. Don't play." Nor had he said, "No problem, play away."

Noel understood the underlying message, however. And sold his precious boots.

After the prayer meeting one Friday night, Billy Balmer had a proposal to put to the keen new Christian. "I would like you to consider becoming a Sunday School teacher, Noel," he said.

"Oh, I could never do that!" was Noel's instant and instinctive reply.

"And why not? How do you know you couldn't? Sure you have never even tried it!" Billy wasn't going to be easily put off.

Despite all Noel's protests about being 'far too young', and there being lots of others who had been Christians for longer than he had who could do it, Billy refused to take 'No' for an answer.

While Noel resisted he insisted.

Then, eventually, since Billy persisted, Noel relented.

"O.K. then, I will give it a try," he agreed, somewhat apprehensively.

Billy sighed, and smiled, all at once. "Great!" he said. "I know you will be a good teacher." He was glad that he had been able to persuade this promising young man to take on a Sunday School class. But it had taken a lot of time, patience, and effort!

It was by now early Saturday morning!

In 1963, and less than a year since he had come to the Saviour, Noel Stevenson began teaching in the Sunday School in Ravenhill Free Presbyterian Church. And he enjoyed it. Loved it. For it brought a different dimension, a spiritual focus, into his life.

This opportunity to take responsibility for a Sunday School class helped the new teacher in two distinct ways. In addition to allowing him to share his faith with, and present the Gospel to, the children in his class, it proved to be a spiritual lifeline to him. When temptation came his way, when Satan tried to tell him that he was a fool, that he could still be enjoying himself if he returned to his former pursuits, the thought of the children in his Sunday School class kept him going. I can't let God, or my class, or myself, down, was his unspoken reply to such recurring temptations.

The Sunday School was Noel's introduction to Christian work. It wasn't long until he became involved in other avenues of outreach. The Children's Meeting, open-air work, and tract distribution. There was developing within him an ever increasing desire to be useful for God.

Highlights of his life were when missionaries like Victor Maxwell, Emma Munn or Bill Woods came home to Northern Ireland on furlough, and told of the wonderful ways in which God was blessing His work overseas.

Bill Woods returned, on furlough, from Brazil, in the late summer of 1964, and gave a number of missionary reports. Noel never missed an opportunity to hear him. Now twenty years of age, he packed in, with hundreds of others, to hear the missionary recount exciting stories of blessing in salvation. The atmosphere was always electric in those meetings. The attention absolute. And nobody seemed to care how long they went on. They just wanted to hear more and more!

Noel was challenged by God through the life and work of Bill Woods. To him he was a modern-day C.T. Studd or Hudson Taylor. A spiritual star. A twentieth-century Christian hero. Giving up everything to go and labour for God in the jungles of Brazil.

As the years passed Noel became increasingly convinced that he was missing out on the will of God for his life. He was employed, at that time, in the Camco factory, in Newtownabbey, on the outskirts of Belfast. Tending his machine, hour after hour, he used to ask himself frequently, "Is this all there is to life? Am I going to have to work here all the rest of my days, and do nothing worthwhile for God?" When thoughts like that beseiged his mind, Noel used to slip behind the machine and wipe away a tear.

He so much wanted to serve God. Somehow, somewhere, see souls won for the Saviour. But he needed to work. He was now married and had a wife and four children to support. How could he ever afford to go to College and train for anything?

What could he do?

He was challenged one day, during his own daily Bible reading at home. In his personal quiet time with God. The reading was from the Book of Nehemiah. It was about how Nehemiah had enlisted volunteers to rebuild the walls of Jerusalem.

Suddenly, almost involuntarily, Noel exclaimed in frustration, "If I had been living in your day, Nehemiah, I would have helped you to build those walls!"

Almost as suddenly as he had cried out, an answer seemed to come back. To his soul. From God. "What about now?" it said. "Are you not going to do anything for me, **now?**"

Thinking that it would be an effective way in which to serve the community, and contact needy souls for Christ, Noel applied for the Prison Service. And was interviewed. By two men and a lady.

After discussing his application with him, the interviewing panel asked Noel about the level of his church involvement. The applicant told them of his work in the Sunday School, the Children's Meeting, and the open-air witness.

The first man remarked, after Noel had finished, "You know, Mr. Stevenson, we would be stopping you in that work. Not because you would have to stop it, but your shift patterns would rule it out."

The other man had lit a cigarette. He put his head back and studiously blew perfect smoke-rings. Then he spoke. "Do you know what I think, Mr. Stevenson?" he said, with the air of a judge summing up the case. "You would be better on the outside than the inside, for with all this work you are doing you might just stop some of these boys coming in to us."

That was it.

Noel knew that the door to the Prison Service was closed. And bolted.

God had shut it. Fast.

Shortly after that, one Sunday morning in the Martyrs Memorial Free Presbyterian Church, Dr. Paisley thumped the pulpit. "This Church needs a full-time children's evangelist," he announced, with mighty conviction.

Noel Stevenson was sitting in the back seat. All at once his heart flipped over.

Was this it? Was this what God wanted him to do? He loved the Sunday School. He loved the children's meetings. He enjoyed working with young people of all ages...

When he arrived home for lunch that Sunday, Noel said to his wife, "Marie, Dr. Paisley made an appeal in the service this morning for a full-time children's evangelist. I feel I should answer that call."

Aware that his wife was about to make some comment, Noel forestalled her. He had something more to say. It was important that she knew all the facts. Was under no illusions. "Before you say anything, Marie," he continued, "do you realize that if I take this on your housekeeping allowance will be cut drastically? Maybe by as much as fifty per cent."

Marie knew how much her husband had longed to serve God, full-time. And she was willing to support him, whatever the cost. "If you think God is calling you, Noel, you do it. If He is calling you, He will look after us," she replied.

Before going to Dr. Paisley to tell him of his willingness to undertake the work, Noel wanted to be absolutely sure that it was the right thing to do. So he decided to consult six of the senior men of the Church. Men whose spiritual integrity he respected. He approached each of these men, separately, and asked them the same set of questions. "Do you think Dr. Paisley really means this? Is there an opening for a full-time children's evangelist in this Church? Will you pray about it for me?"

Each one of those men, unaware that any of the others had been contacted, gave him the same answer. "When I heard that appeal being made, I thought about you, Noel. Yes I will pray for you, but I think you should consider taking it on."

So Noel prayed. And Marie prayed. And those six church leaders prayed.

Then Noel made up his mind. He would do it. For God.

Now he had to tell Dr. Paisley.

He was just going to do that every Sunday. But every Sunday for six weeks he came home annoyed with himself. Unfulfilled. He hadn't been able to pluck up the courage to tell him. Made excuses for himself, that he had never found a suitable opportunity.

Then came the Church Social. Dr. Paisley preached very forcefully about Moses standing still at the Red Sea. "Moses stood still, but God said, 'Go forward!' We must all go forward for God!" he thundered, punching the air emphatically.

Noel sat there. Convicted, again.

"Tonight I go forward," he resolved.

And he did..

During the supper, afterwards, Noel went to Dr. Paisley and said, simply, "I would like to respond to the call you made one Sunday morning a month or two ago. I think I would like to become a children's evangelist in this Church."

Dr. Paisley was pleased. "That's great, Noel," he replied. "We will put you through the College." With his first words, and all in one breath, he had swept away the obstacle that had been keeping Noel back from serving the Lord for years!

In September, 1978, Noel was interviewed by the Church session and duly appointed as Children's Evangelist. More than ten years of spiritual agony were over.

For the past twenty years Noel Stevenson has served God faithfully in Martyr's Memorial Free Presbyterian Church. In that time he has seen hundreds of children presented with the message of the Gospel, and many saved.

A fitting tribute to his work for God, and the esteem in which he is held in the Church, is is one of the plaques in the hallway of the new Paisley Jubilee complex, telling of a foundation stone that was laid, amongst a number of others, on Easter Monday, 31st March, 1997.

The plaque states that a foundation stone was laid, 'by Noel Stevenson, Youth Evangelist, on behalf of the Youth Workers, and the Church's youth. 2 Timothy 3 v 15.'

Noel has no doubt whatsoever that he has made the best possible use of his life. For God. And the youth of Belfast.

14

TELL YOUR CHILDREN ...

❖

D r. Paisley and his wife Eileen have five of a family. And all five, as children, had tender hearts. They were used to lives lived in the fear and in the presence of God. The Bible was read aloud to them in the home every day. And they heard either daddy, or mummy, or both, praying for them each one as individuals. Praying that they would be saved and live a life to the glory of God.

So it is probably not surprising then, that they all came to know the Saviour, early in life.

When Sharon, the eldest of the five, was very young, her mummy used to take her up on her knee and read stories from the Bible to her. Once, when the story was about the crucifixion of the Lord Jesus, her mummy noticed the chubby fists go up one after another to her cheeks. She was smudging away the tears.

One night, when she was four years old, Sharon came down the stairs, very sheepishly. She was dead scared that she would be sent straight back up again.

"I just came down for a wee drink of water," was her excuse.

Mummy poured her the drink of water, then watched as she sat on the edge of a chair, dangling her legs. Playing with the glass, rather than drinking the water.

Then came the truth. The real reason for her appearance in the living-room. "Mummy, I didn't really come down for a drink of water. I came down to get saved," she said, quietly.

"Are you sure, dear ?" Her mummy was pleased, but didn't want to push her young daughter too hard too soon.

"Yes, Mummy, I'm sure." Little Sharon was determined. She knew what she wanted.

So, very simply, Mrs. Paisley pointed her eldest child to Christ. And very simply, Sharon trusted in Him.

As her mummy was tucking her up in bed, later on, Sharon looked up from below the covers and declared, "I'm happy now, Mummy. I'm happy."

She was, too. And she showed it.

As eldest member of the family, Sharon became the example, the role model, for the others. She was third in their order of Very Important People. First was God. Then second, as kind of equals, were daddy and mummy. Then came Sharon.

Rhonda loved her big sister. They were great friends. And she too was often moved by the Bible stories. One day she had obviously been thinking about the story of the cross. Out of the blue she remarked to her mum, with a very sad expression, "Poor Jesus. That must have been very terrible sore. If I had been there I would have fixed them!"

Even though not yet a Christian herself, Rhonda wasn't a bit afraid to speak out about spiritual things. There were two questions that she used to ask anyone who came about the house, if she could corner them somewhere, somehow. And there was no particular pattern, either, as to who she questioned, or when or how often she conducted her enquiries.

The two questions were, "Are you saved?", and, "Do you go to my Daddy's church?"

You were in favour with Rhonda if you were saved. But if you went to her 'Daddy's church' as well, you were just great! You had made it in life! What more could anybody want?!

When she was eight years old, Rhonda went along with the rest of the family to a meeting in the Ulster Hall. An American evangelist, Dr. Bob Wells, was preaching.

Rhonda was convicted by the Spirit of God in that meeting. She realized that despite saying all the right things and asking all the right questions, she wasn't right with God herself.

At the end of the meeting, as the appeal was being made, she cried out, aloud, "Oh mummy, I'm not saved!"

Having become acutely aware of her condition, Rhonda also knew the solution. She went forward into the enquiry room, and was pointed to the Lord.

The third member of the family, Cherith, also responded to the invitation of Jesus, 'Suffer the little children to come unto me, and forbid them not,' as a young child.

One night, as she was preparing for bed, she asked a very important question. It was, "Mummy, can I get saved tonight?"

"Yes, indeed you can, dear," was the glad reponse to that sincere enquiry.

Then, after her mum had spoken to her about what it meant to be saved, Cherith, in childlike faith, came to Christ.

That only left the twins, Ian and Kyle still unsaved...

On a Sunday night in April, 1971, Mrs. Paisley brought the children home from the evening service and saw them all off to bed. Then, as Dr. Paisley and she had to go out again to separate engagements, she left them in charge of a babysitter.

Much later, when she returned home, Mrs. Paisley found the babysitter a bit worried. "Ian is crying up there in bed. I just couldn't get him to settle at all," she reported.

When his mum went up to the bedroom, she spoke softly to Ian. It was hard to know whether his brother, Kyle, was sound asleep, as he appeared to be, or just faking.

"What's wrong, Ian, son?" she asked. "Are you not very well?"

"Oh I'm all right. I'm not sick," he sobbed in response. "But I wanted to get saved tonight in church. I put my hand up, but daddy didn't see it. I really want to be saved."

When she had spoken to him for a little while to calm him down a bit, his mum had the thrill of hearing young Ian confess Christ as his Saviour.

Next morning the little lad, full of the joy of salvation, went into school and told his friends, and the teacher, that he was saved. He was a Christian, now.

Dr. Paisley had been away overnight, and when he came home, late on Monday afternoon, his wife told him about young Ian's conversion. "Praise God. That's wonderful," was his immediate reaction. "And what about Kyle?"

"Oh he didn't say anything and I didn't push him," Mrs. Paisley replied.

"I will speak to the both of them," he volunteered.

Later on that evening, the man who had preached the Gospel to thousands in his lifetime, sat down with his twin sons. "Tell me all about what happened last night, Ian," he began.

"Last night I asked Jesus into my heart, daddy," was the straightforward answer to that one.

"That's great, son," his dad replied. Then turning to his other son, he went on, "And what about you, Kyle?"

"I didn't trust in Jesus last night. But I would like to," he answered, shyly. Solemnly.

"If you really mean it, Kyle, you come with me and we will talk about it," dad said, rising.

Kyle did mean it, so both of them retired to another room. In there, in the stillness, the minister who was used to telling large, attentive audiences about the love of God, the death of Christ and salvation for the 'whosoever will', told that same message to his small attentive son. And Kyle, too, was saved.

Now they were a family united in Christ.

Rejoicing in salvation.

Prepared to serve the Lord.

... AND YOUR CHILDREN'S CHILDREN.

John and Sharon's little daughter, Lydia, had been sitting thoughtfully for a while one afternoon. Then she let her mummy into the secret of what was on her mind.

"Mummy, I'm going to die. Because I'm not saved, I'm going to die," she said. "I want to get saved."

They sat together, mother and daughter, and Sharon pointed Lydia, the eldest of the Paisley grandchildren, to the Lord.

Shortly after, Lydia went into her bedroom. On coming out again, about ten minutes later, she declared, "I'm saved and going to heaven. I'm happy now."

She knew that the joy she was experiencing was of the infectious nature. It would make her grandparents happy, too. So she rang up.

"Nana, I have just asked Jesus into my heart," she announced, as soon as Mrs. Paisley answered. Then almost in the same breath she went on, "Is Papa there?"

"No, he's not, love," Nana told her."But you will get him on his mobile."

She rang off, happily.

Fifteeen minutes later Mrs. Paisley had another call from her little granddaughter. She was more frustrated than excited, now.

"Nana, I can't get through on that old mobile phone of Papa's. It's always engaged," she complained.

Nana chuckled quietly. She knew the feeling.

"Just keep trying, dear. You will get through to him eventually," was her advice, born out of years of experience.

Lydia kept trying. And Nana had been right. She did get through to Papa eventually.

When she told him that she had 'trusted in Jesus', her Papa replied, "I'm really glad to hear that, Lydia. Tell me what happened. Did Jesus come into your heart?"

Adults can be so simple. So stupid about things, at times.

"Of course He did, Papa," she retorted, immediately, "He said He would. Didn't He?!"

When Shane Caldwell, Cherith's son, arrived home from Nursery School one afternoon, he had something special to tell his mummy. Not about School. But about himself.

"Mummy, I asked Jesus into my heart today," he informed her.

"Did you Shane? That's great!" Cherith was delighted. "Tell me what happened."

"Jesus came in and washed my sins away," he replied, simply.

When his daddy arrived home from work, Shane told him about it. Daddy was delighted, too. Then he wanted to tell Nana and Papa. So Andrew and Cherith brought him over to their house.

When they heard the news, 'back at home', they were all thrilled. Everybody had something encouraging to say. Or, indeed, some question to ask.

Aunt Rhonda enquired, "What does it mean that you are saved, Shane?"

"It means that Jesus is in my heart, and I'm going to heaven. That's where that old Devil man will never be," was her nephew's summary of salvation.

His aunt laughed. Then gave him a big hug.

She couldn't have explained it any better herself!

In January, 1998, Dr. Paisley and his wife, Eileen, went to see their most recent grandchild for the first time. Their son Kyle and daughter-in-law Janice already had Kara and Danielle. Now this was their third daughter, Bethany.

Before they arrived, Kara, the oldest of the three girls, told her daddy, "I have asked Jesus into my heart." This good news was soon reported to the loving, praying grandparents.

So, when visiting, Nana took the opportunity to ask her granddaughter, "Is it right, Kara, that you have asked Jesus into your heart? Are you saved?"

"Yes, Nana," she replied, without hesitation. "I did ask Jesus into my heart. I'm saved."

And she knew what she was talking about, too.

One day she had a question for her daddy. Children sometimes get fed up answering questions. They like to ask one or two of their own now and again.

"What do you think of Jesus, daddy?" she wanted to know.

"Oh, I love Him," her dad replied at once.

"Yes. And I know why you love Him. You love Him because He loved you first."

She was right!

Ian, junior, and his wife Fiona, have two little daughters, Emily and Lucy, who are both still very young. The whole family circle, and indeed a much wider circle of Christian friends, are all praying that they, along with Janice and Kyle's two younger daughters, may come to know the Saviour early in life.

What a wonderful blessing that would be. To see the entire family circle united in Christ!

Rejoicing in salvation.

Prepared to serve the Lord.

15

PEGGY AND TED

❖

One day, at work, Bob Cathcart was discussing the political situation in Northern Ireland with his mate, Ted Ashby.

"You and Peggy ought to come along with me to hear Ian Paisley in the Ulster Hall sometime," he suggested. "I think you would like him."

When Ted went home and told Peggy of Bob's invitation, the idea appealed to her. So they went along.

Ted and Peggy were impressed with the big man from the very first time they heard him. His fire. His enthusiasm. His knowledge. Indeed, they found something compelling about his whole personality.

A few months later, Bob Cathcart, who was not at that time a Christian himself, had another suggestion to make. "Why don't you go along some Sunday evening to the Ulster Hall and hear Dr. Paisley preach the Gospel?" he ventured.

So they began to do that, too.

For the first few meetings, though, it didn't register with them that this was any different from any other rally. They were there to hear the man. Not heed the message.

Although the Ashbys then lived in Mountainview Drive, off the Crumlin Road, they were members of a city centre Parish Church, and attended on occasional Sunday mornings.

On one such Sunday afternoon, however, Peggy became incensed. Angry. Mad. She had started to read the little church magazine which had been given to her that morning. And in it she discovered an article, criticising Ian Paisley for opening an Orange Arch in Brown Square.

As it so happened, a few weeks later, a lady worker from the church called to ask if Ted and Peggy would consider making some sort of a financial pledge to the church.

Peggy seized what she saw as her opportunity. "I won't be making any pledge to that church until I have seen the minister," she stormed. "Ask him to call round and see me, sometime."

Next week the minister arrived to visit. He wasn't long into the house until Peggy told him of her disgust at the magazine article. For two hours the minister stayed with her, drinking tea, and smoking the occasional cigarette. And explaining why Ian Paisley could never be a REAL minister, since he had never been to University.

Peggy informed him that Dr. Ian Paisley *was* a REAL minister, because, "... he tells the people how to get saved."

"Oh you don't need to worry about all that stuff about being saved," he went on. "As long as you live a kind and honest life, and love God and your neighbour you will be O.K.. Our God is a God of love, you know."

Although not saved herself, Peggy was appalled. She knew she needed to be saved, and so did everybody else as well.

As the minister left, Peggy informed him that she and Ted would never be back to his church.

But what were they going to do? They were church-going types and felt they should be going out somewhere on a Sunday.

One Saturday morning they went up the Ravenhill Road and found

Dr. Paisley in attendance at Ravenhill Free Presbyterian Church. After recounting their previous experiences, they asked, "Would it be all right if we came along to your services every week?"

"It certainly would", was Dr. Paisley's immediate reply. Then he added, "And I hope it won't be long until I am leading you both to the Lord!"

Thus it was that Ted and Peggy Ashby became regular attenders at as many meetings as they could manage, conducted by Dr. Paisley.

One Sunday morning, in early February, 1968, Ted had to go to work, so Peggy went along to the Ulster Hall meeting, with her son, Alastair. Since Peggy didn't want to miss a single word of anything, they sat right up at the front.

As a torrent of spiritual wisdom and advice flowed from the preacher on the platform, she gazed up at him. Transfixed. Hanging on every word. To her, he was just great. She loved his style. Forthright. Full of zeal for God. Pulling no punches.

But that particular morning proved to be different from all the other mornings when she had attended. For on that morning the message got beyond her head. And her happy hero-worship.

It penetrated right into her heart and soul.

The theme of the address was the assurance of salvation. It was intended for Christians. How they could be sure that they were saved. But Peggy wasn't saved at all. And knew she needed to be.

She had been busy telling everybody about 'the great man' she went to hear, and the great meetings, and the great messages... But she had never taken the message of the Gospel to herself.

She had never come to the Saviour.

She had never been to the cross.

At the close of that service, Dr. Paisley made an appeal. That was unusual. It wasn't his normal way of ending a meeting for believers, but on that morning he was convinced that the Spirit of God was at work on an unsaved heart, somewhere in the gathering.

He asked, from the platform, "If there is anybody here, still not saved, and would like to be saved this morning, just raise your hand. That won't save you , but it will allow us to identify you. Then we can read the Scriptures with you, and point you to Christ."

Peggy Ashby raised her hand. It seemed that there was some power, beyond her physical control altogether, pushing it up.

She really wanted to be saved, there and then. That very morning.

As the crowds filed out of the Ulster Hall, Peggy remained behind. When almost everybody had gone she was shown into a little room where Dr. Paisley joined her.

Sitting down beside her, he read a series of Bible verses. Peggy recognised some of them, but not all. The one, however, that spoke to her soul was John 3 v 16. 'For God so loved the world, that he gave his only begotten Son, that whosoever believeth in him should not perish, but have everlasting life.'

As she thought on the love of God and the invitation to trust in Christ, Peggy Ashby came simply and humbly, and accepted Him as her Saviour.

Dr. Paisley prayed with her, and she left. Saved. There was a sense of calm and contentment in her soul, that she had never experienced before. Never even believed possible.

After rejoining Alastair, who had been sitting patiently in the main auditorium waiting for his mother's return, they set off for home.

When they arrived back at the house, Peggy could hardly wait until Ted returned from work, to tell him her good news.

As soon he came in, Peggy greeted him with a beaming smile and tears welling up in her eyes. Her first words were, "Ted, I just want to tell you that I got saved in the service this morning."

Ted was patient. And understanding. But he didn't see much sense in becoming 'all worked up' and emotional about religion and salvation and things like that.

"We have been together for so long now, Peggy, we won't let that come between us. If it's what you want and it makes you happy it will be all right with me." was his measured response.

It was 'all right' with him for Peggy to be saved, if that was the sort of thing she wanted. Yet he determined, inwardly, that all this talk about 'being saved' and 'being born again' was just a lot of sentimental hype and it wasn't for him.

There were two factors that he hadn't reckoned upon, though. One was the power of prayer and the other was the working of the

Holy Spirit. From the moment that she was saved, Peggy began to pray earnestly for her husband. That he, too, would soon experience the joy of God's salvation. And so did dozens of others in the Ravenhill Free Presbyterian Church.

Although Ted wasn't saved, nor did he even show any particicular interest in being saved, he had one absorbing hobby. Something to which he devoted a great deal of his leisure time. It was his tape recorder. He owned a big reel-to-reel tape recorder, and he just relished any possible opportunity to use it.

Peggy brought Ted along to every meeting she could in the church.

Ted, in turn, brought along his constant companion. His tape-recorder. And recorded the messages. Then he made copies for anybody who wanted them.

During the summer of 1968, Ted had gone across, with other members of his Orange Lodge, to hear Dr. Paisley speak at an Orange service in Kirkintilloch, Scotland. Always glad of a chance to record something, where there was obviously going to be a demand for repeat tapes, he had his recorder with him.

A few weeks after he arrived home, Ted had a number of orders for copies of the tape of that service. Both from people in Northern Ireland and in Scotland.

So he set to work.

One day he was working away in the spare bedroom that doubled as his 'recording studio'. The bed had been converted into his work-bench. Bulky machines and boxes of tapes occupied every available space.

It was only when he had almost completed the operation that he realized that he was going to end up short of one blank tape. He needed to make three more copies, but he had only two blank tapes left.

There was an easy solution to that problem. One he had often used before. Recycling. He would record over a used tape that was no longer required.

Ted picked up a ribbon tape of Dr. Bob Jones whom he had recorded on an earlier visit to Belfast. 'The very thing', he thought. 'That will do. I have made as many recordings of that one as I will ever need now'.

Before taping over Dr. Jones, however, Ted decided to find out what was on that tape. Out of curiosity. So he started to play snippets of it, fast-forwarding it every now and again.

He was just aimlessly fiddling about. Or so he thought!

As the tape came near to, but not quite at, the end, the machine jammed. Stuck.

Part of the appeal at the end of the service filled the bedroom. Time and time again. It was the church congregation singing, softly,

'Just as I am, without one plea,
But that Thy blood was shed for me,
And that Thou bidst me come to Thee,
O Lamb of God, I come, I come.'

Ted tried to free it.

He rewound the tape a bit, to relieve the jam.

And started to play it again.

Again it stuck. At the very same place.

The verse of the hymn was repeated over and over again. Again...

'Just as I am, without one plea...'

Ted was becoming frustrated.

He rewound the tape once more. It shouldn't be sticking. He couldn't discover any technical reason why the thing was sticking at that particular spot.

He replayed it. A third time.

Surely it would work properly now.

But no. It didn't.

Yet again the soft singing soothed its way into that bedroom.

'Just as I am, witout one plea,
But that Thy blood was shed for me...'

This time Ted wasn't frustrated.

Like young Samuel so long ago, he was forced to the conclusion that God was trying to get through to him. To tell him something.

He was convicted.

Kneeling down at one of the few vacant spaces at the bedside, he poured out his heart to God. "Lord, I can't understand why this is happening, but I know it must be for me," he prayed. "I know I need

You, Lord. I am coming now to You. Thank You Lord, for dying for me. Please take away my sin. And take me as I am."

Ted Ashby was saved.

When he went downstairs and told Peggy she was overjoyed. Her God had answered her many prayers. And now her Saviour had become her husband's Saviour too.

Ted never did reuse that tape. It was never taped over. For many years, though, he used his interest, and his equipment for the Lord. He recorded Dr. Paisley's sermons every Sunday and distributed copies to housebound and elderly people both in Northern Ireland and mainland Britain.

Peggy had a talent that she too could use for God. She could make tea!

After they were saved she and Ted heard of a struggling outreach work in the Duff Memorial Hall, in the Sandy Row district of Belfast. In 1970 there were only about four people going in there every Thursday night.

Peggy suggested to 'Herbie' Webb, an old veteran of The First World War, who organised the work, that she would make a cup of tea for everybody, every Thursday night. She wanted to do something simple, and practical, for the Lord.

And it worked !

The people of Sandy Row must have liked their cup of tea, for as the Christians prayed, and the tea was served, the numbers attending gradually began to increase.

God has blessed Peggy and Ted in their faithful service for Him in that area, for almost thirty years. Souls have been saved, one of the most notable being Tommy Sherlock, who now helps in the meetings, and Christians have been encouraged.

And they haven't retired from that work yet, either.

They are still there.

Humbly serving God. He means so much to them.

16

A LITTLE CHILD SHALL
LEAD THEM

❖

Late in 1968, Mrs. Paisley's housekeeper told her that she was leaving. The busy city councillor was disappointed. This young woman had been great with the children, but the reason she gave for moving on was totally understandable. She was planning to undertake a course of full-time study leading to a qualification in child-care.

Away on the other side of the city, the newly- converted couple, Peggy and Ted Ashby, heard of this situation. And they believed they had the answer.

Ted called with Mrs. Paisley one day, and said, "We have heard that your housekeeper is leaving. Well, I think we know somebody who could take her place. Peggy's sister, a Mrs. Bennett, has worked for years as a housekeeper to a doctor in Holywood. This doctor has just retired there a couple of months ago, and now she is out of a job. We are sure she would be good."

"That sounds great. Just the sort of person I need. Somebody mature to look after the children," was Mrs. Paisley's immediate response. "Send her over some time and we can have a chat about it."

Vera Bennett called at the Paisley home on a Friday, and she and her prospective new employer liked each other right from that very first encounter. The two women 'just clicked'.

So on the following Monday, Mrs Bennett took up her position as housekeeper to the Paisley family. Little did she know then, though, of what exactly she had let herself in for! How, and by whom, God was going to challenge her! And lead her to Himself.

In addition to her household chores, a vital part of Mrs. Bennett's duties was to take care of the children. The two older girls, Sharon and Rhonda, were at School during the day, but Vera soon realized that she 'had her hands full' with the three who were left. They were the nearly-four-year-old Cherith, and the twins, Ian and Kyle, who were younger still.

Since the children were so very young, Mrs. Bennett spent a lot of time with them. Supervising them. Talking to them. Checking that the boys, especially, didn't conjure up any mischief. And answering the seemingly endless barrage of questions...

One thing that soon struck Vera about little Cherith was that she seemed to be so happy and pleasant for most of the time. She nearly always seemed to be singing something.

As all four of them were together one afternoon, the housekeeper, who by now they all adored, remarked on this, to Cherith.

"You are a very happy little girl, Cherith", she said, with an admiring smile. "You are always singing!"

"Yes, I am happy, Mrs. Bennett", the little one replied at once. "I will sing you about being happy."

Whereupon she launched forth into song. Into a chorus which she had learnt in Sunday School...

> *"You ask me why I'm happy,*
> *So I'll just tell you why,*
> *Because my sins are gone.*
> *They're underneath the blood*
> *Of the cross of Calvary,*

As far removed as darkness is from dawn.
In the sea of God's forgetfulness,
That's good enough for me,
Praise God my sins are gone."

As soon as she had fnished singing, Cherith looked up at the kind and caring woman and asked, innocently, "Are your sins gone, Mrs. Bennett?"

Tears brimmed up in the housekeeper's eyes. Then they started to trickle slowly down her cheeks.

"No, dear," she was forced to concede, at length. "My sins aren't gone."

The twins had been listening to their big sister's solo effort. And the ensuing conversation.

Kyle, though still very young, had been well taught in the truth. Nor had he any hesitation about sharing it. He piped up, "Mrs. Bennett, you know that if you want to go to heaven, you need to be saved."

Not to be outdone, young Ian thought that he ought to get his pennyworth in too, so he followed on. To deliver the knockout punch. "Mrs. Bennett, do you really WANT to go to hell?" he enquired.

"No, love, indeed I don't," the by now feeling-somewhat-beleagured lady replied. And then hastily changed the subject.

But there was no getting away from it. Vera Bennett had learnt something, something very important, from the children in her competent care.

She had discovered the personal nature of salvation. She had learnt that if she ever wanted to be in heaven, then her sins would have to be gone.

She would have to come to Christ, herself. Get to the cross of Calvary. And trust the dying Saviour.

A few months later, one evening as Mrs. Bennett was preparing to go home, at the end of her day's work, she turned to Mrs. Paisley. "You know, your husband ought to be proud of Cherith," she said.

Mrs. Paisley was a bit puzzled. "Why? What do you mean?" she asked.

"I mean she is after my soul!" was the housekeeper's reply.

Feeling a little bit embarrassed, in case the good woman was feeling harrassed in her home, and a big bit responsible for her actively-witnessing daughter, Cherith's mum assured her, " You can be sure we don't tell her to say anything to you, Mrs. Bennett."

"Oh, indeed I know that Mrs. Paisley!" she retorted. "You can soon tell when children have been primed. No, Cherith is so natural about it. So very sincere, in her own little way."

One of those natural and sincere pieces of information that Cherith let out one day really went straight to her minder's heart. "You know Mrs. Bennett, my mammy and daddy pray for you and your family every day at our family prayer time", she said.

That touched the housekeeper. Got to her.

She realized from what Cherith had told her that she was more than just a servant in their household. She was a cherished member of the family. Somebody they all cared about enough to pray for every day.

Good news for Cherith came one Friday afternoon. Just as Mrs. Bennett was preparing to go off for the weekend she said to her little charge, "Do you know where I'm going on Sunday, Cherith? I'm going to your church to hear your daddy preaching."

Cherith replied, "Oh good, Mrs. Bennett. Will you get saved?"

"Now don't push me, child," Mrs. Bennett chuckled. "I have promised to go to the church to hear your daddy. Let's leave it at that." They had to. For the housekeeper set off for home.

Vera kept her promise. She arrived at the Martyrs Memorial Free Presbyterian Church on the Ravenhill Road, on the Sunday night. To hear Cherith's 'daddy preaching.'

True to his usual style Cherith's daddy preached the Gospel. But Mrs. Bennett had heard it all before. In his home. From his children. And when the appeal was made at the close of the message she was the first one up the aisle!

Dr. Paisley saw her making her way forward and nodded to his wife, Eileen, to go into the enquiry room.

When Mrs. Paisley saw the housekeeper whom they all loved so much, and had prayed for so regularly, coming into the little room she could just hardly take it in. It all seemed so unreal, somehow.

It wasn't difficult to point Mrs. Bennett to the Lord. The groundwork had been laid by Cherith and the twins. And she had been convicted by the power of the Holy Spirit.

After Mrs. Bennett had come to Christ she and her employer, who was now her spiritual counsellor, rejoiced together.

When she arrived home later on, Vera Bennett told her husband and family of her salvation. And as a result of her testimony, her son John started to attend the services in the Martyr's Memorial Church, and he also was saved.

It was late in the evening when Mrs. Paisley tiptoed into Cherith's bedroom. The little girl was asleep.

A few moments later she seemed to stir.

"Do you know what happened tonight, Cherith?" her mum whispered. "Mrs. Bennett got saved."

Rubbing her eyes, and still barely awake, Cherith replied, in an almost matter-of-fact tone, "Sure I know that."

The ways and minds of children could be hard to understand sometimes, but with five of a family Eileen Paisley reckoned that she was pretty good at figuring them out. She was absolutely baffled by this one, however. Cherith hadn't been to the service. Nobody had come home earlier to tell her anything of what had happened. How could she know? There was only one way to find out...

"And how did you know, dear?" she enquired, softly.

Cherith was wakening up by now and becoming increasingly exasperated with all these adult-type probing questions.

Her reply was a revelation. A wonderful example of, what the Saviour described as 'the faith of a little child.'

"Before I came to bed I asked Jesus to do that, and He said He would!" she declared.

What faith!

What an effective witness!

What a wonderful God!

17

THREE BOOKLETS
FOR TWO BOB

❖

Tiger Bay is a 'loyalist' area of North Belfast. Rows of little
streets run off rows of other little streets. The people there, in
the early 1960's, were fiercely Protestant. And it was in that
environment that Trevor Baxter grew up.

Throughout his early teenage years, Trevor never missed a band
parade. Or a chance to show off his prowess as a ringleader in bad-
ness.

He wasn't at all worried about what he said. How he said it. Or to
whom he said it.

Nor was he worried, either, about what he stole. How he stole it.
Or from whom he stole it.

One evening, the young tearaway was watching the T.V. news.
Suddenly the screen seemed to be filled with this larger-than-life
figure, wearing a round collar. The man-on-the-screen was holding
forth vociferously on some issue or other. And what he said
pleased the young Trevor Baxter. It was his opinion on the matter,
precisely.

Sitting there in the family living-room, Trevor made a resolution. That very minute. "If that man is a minister," he promised himself, "I am going to find his church. And hear what he has to say."

When he had made a few enquiries, Trevor Baxter, aged seventeen, discovered that the man whom he had seen on the T.V. news was called Ian Paisley. He was the minister of a church across in the south of the city. Up the Ravenhill Road somewhere.

So, very soon, he set off on his motor-bicycle to try and find the church. After a few exploratory runs around the district it didn't take him long to locate the building and learn that it was called Ravenhill Free Presbyterian Church.

When he first heard the fiery character whom he had seen on T.V., preach the Gospel, Trevor was amazed to discover that there was this experience called 'salvation', which he knew nothing whatsoever about. Although he had gone to church in his earlier days, and had been a member of the Boy's Brigade, he had never been made aware of his need of a Saviour.

His ignorance of things spiritual, was total.

As well as being startled by what he heard, Trevor was also struck by the obvious sincerity of the big man who was saying it. Never before had he heard anybody preach with the same conviction, the same fiery devotion, as this minister. He was really in earnest. He seemed fully persuaded in his own mind that what he was telling his audience was important. Vitally, immediately and eternally important.

Trevor started to attend Ravenhill Free Presbyterian Church every Sunday. Not, at that stage, because he was convicted by the preaching. But he was captivated by the preacher.

It wasn't long until Trevor became an ardent follower of Rev. Ian Paisley, never missing any opportunity to hear him speak, whether in a Sunday service or at a rally or parade. The powerful personality of the man, combined with his fearlessly presented political persuasions, attracted the teenager like a magnet. And although he had become more politically alive, Trevor still remained spiritually dead. Not saved.

However, as he continued to attend Rev. Paisley's church on the Ravenhill Road every Sunday, he soon realized that there was a difference between himself and those all around him. Most of the others at the meetings seemed to have something which was patently lacking in his life. They were kind, considerate, friendly, and welcoming. They all seemed so deep-down inwardly content, too.

He had never heard any of them swear. And he could nearly be sure that they wouldn't steal, either.

He would have to reform. Clean up his act a bit. Look the part.

So he tried to stop the swearing. Vowed, also, that he would never steal anything, again. Ever.

Then, just to complete the image, 'make the sweet complete', he bought a 'Jesus Saves' badge to wear. And wore it.

Trevor still wasn't saved, though.

The message on his new, shiny lapel badge was absolutely true. Jesus did, could, and would, save.

But He hadn't saved Trevor. Yet.

Not because He didn't want to. But because Trevor wasn't willing. Yet.

Every time he went along to Ravenhill Free Presbyterian Church to hear his hero speak, Trevor heard the Gospel. And at many of the outdoor rallies, too. There appeared to be no way of escaping it! Rev. Paisley never seemed to miss any opportunity to inform people of their need of Christ.

In the autumn of 1966, Trevor attended a rally in Ballymena, and, out of interest, bought three booklets. They were a special offer pack. Three for two shillings. (10p) Not bad value, he decided. Anyway, he would never miss 'the two bob bit.' The florin.

One of the booklets was a sermon by Rev. Paisley, 'Jesus Christ, Not Able To Sin', the second was a report of the preacher's recent visit to Rome, and the other was entitled, 'In These Last Days', by Fred Hamilton and Cecil McKay.

When he arrived home from that rally, late in the evening, Trevor read the three booklets, and then put them away. Not really planning to ever read them again...

On the morning of Saturday, 5th November, 1966, Trevor was alone in the living-room. Indeed, alone in the house.

Suddenly he felt the urge to read the booklet about 'these last days', once more. There were some ideas in it that were new to him, on the first reading. So he found it. And settled down to read.

As he perused that little book, all that Trevor had been hearing for months came rushing, pouring, flooding, back into his mind. Like a bolt from the blue, the thought arrested him, 'I'm trying to live a Christian life, and I'm not even a Christian. I'm not saved at all. I am only putting on a kind of a show for these people'.

So shattering was this realization, that he decided to do something about it.

At once. There and then. Straightaway.

Slipping down onto his knees at the chair on which he had been sitting, Trevor Baxter, just turned eighteen years of age, accepted Christ as his Saviour. Simply and humbly he confessed his sins, the evils of the long-gone days, and the hypocrisy of the not-so-long-gone days, and asked God to save him.

And He did. That moment.

Salvation brought immediate joy and peace into Trevor's heart and life.

Now he was sure that he was saved. He didn't have to live up to anything any more. Jesus had come into his heart. He was now born of God. And his immediate response was to throw himself wholeheartedly into outreach work.

Trevor soon became involved in many of the activities of the church. He taught in the Sunday School, helped in the children's work, spoke at open-air meetings.

God had effected such a miracle of transformation in his own life that he wanted everybody to know about it. And to find for themselves the wonderful joy and satisfaction that he had experienced.

His parents didn't really know what to make of their son's conversion, at first. They were, just as Trevor had been for eighteen years, not interested in the Bible or things 'religious'. So, although they noticed, and appreciated, the marvellous change in their son's whole demeanour, they just thought that he had become 'a good-living Paisleyite'.

Trevor tried to explain to them that it was God, and not Ian Paisley, Who had brought about the transformation in his life, but they didn't even want to be bothered thinking about such matters. If Trevor liked that sort of stuff, and it kept him out of mischief, that was fair enough for him. But it wasn't for them.

As soon as he was saved, however, Trevor began to pray for his parents. That God would 'open the eyes of their understanding'. That they would, some day, and in some way, despite their apparent apathy, be challenged as to their need of a Saviour. And come to Him by faith.

Four years later, God began to answer those prayers.

In December, 1970, just before Christmas, Trevor's father had a heart attack, and was rushed into the Royal Victoria Hospital.

Since he was deeply concerned both about his father's physical and spiritual condition, Trevor mentioned the matter to Dr. Paisley just after the Sunday evening service in the recently opened Martyrs Memorial Free Presbyterian Church.

"We will go up and see him right now," was the big man's instant response.

So that is what they set out to do.

Dr. Paisley and Trevor drove up to the hospital and made enquiries as to the whereabouts of Mr. Baxter. As Dr. Paisley strode through the corridors, and then the wards, of the hospital, Trevor who was doing his best to keep up with him, was amazed to see nurses and orderlies stopping their work, for a few seconds. To stand and stare. And people who were supposed to be resting with heart conditions, sitting bolt upright in their beds.

"There's Ian Paisley!" they whispered.

But the man whose presence had caused such surprise, paid no notice.

A man was very ill. He might even be in danger of dying. And he wasn't saved. That, to him, was a serious situation.

When the two men eventually located the patient whom they had come to see, the screens were around his bed. Medical staff were moving to and fro, purposefully. They were very busy. Doing what they could for him.

Mr. Baxter was not well enough to receive visitors, they advised.

Not to be deterred, however, Dr. Paisley returned to the hospital the next day. After he had spoken to Trevor's father, the ill man, for whom his son had been praying so earnestly, trusted in Christ as his Saviour. And less than a fortnight later, early in 1971, he passed away. To be in His presence.

Trevor was grieving. But grateful.

God had answered his prayers. He would meet his dad again, one day. In heaven.

In May of that same year, 1971, Trevor was sitting in the living-room of a friend's house with a number of others fom the church.

As the growth of the work at the Martyrs Memorial church was under discussion, Dr. Paisley, who was an experienced Christian-worker-talent-spotter, and one of those present, looked across at the young man, and said, "Trevor, we would like you to consider serving the Lord in a full-time capacity. Here, as an outreach worker, with this church."

Trevor was momentarily taken aback.

The prospect of full-time work of some sort pleased him. It was just exactly what he would love to do. He told Dr. Paisley that he would give it serious consideration.

There were a couple of items that he needed to weigh up in his mind. Practically. One was the fact that he was already working in a well paid job in the Michelin tyre factory at Mallusk, on the outskirts of the city, and he would have to cope with a cut in salary to work in the church. And that possible reduction in income led him to a second possible cause for concern.

He and Mary were engaged to be married. Their wedding date was already set. For August. Could he keep a wife, and then possibly even a family, on an outreach worker's wages?

After a period of prayer and contemplation, he made his decision. And informed Dr. Paisley of it.

He was prepared to serve God, as an outreach worker, in the Martyrs Memorial Free Presbyterian Church. He was convinced that the God Who had saved him, and had kept him for the last five years, could easily provide for his wife and himself. For their family too, for that matter, if He should choose to bless them with one.

So it was that in August, 1971, Trevor and Mary were married, by Dr. Paisley, in the church where Trevor had decided to labour for the Lord.

For four rewarding, but often challenging, years, Trevor Baxter dedicated his love for the Lord and his physical energies, to outreach activities connected to the church. But still he wasn't completely satisfied. He wanted to do even more for God, if possible.

That opportunity, he felt, was in the ministry. So, in 1975, Trevor entered the Theological Hall of the Free Presbyterian Church. To train as a minister. Although they had two children by that time, Trevor and Mary realized that this was a way in which both of them could lay 'their all on the altar' for God.

After four years in College, during which time he also served as a student assistant in Newtownards Free Presbyterian Church, Trevor was ordained as minister in charge of the congregation in Dungannon Free Presbyterian Church, in Co. Tyrone, on 29th November, 1979.

Just thirteen years had elapsed since he had come to the Lord as an eighteen year old. And God had still other blessings to bestow upon His servant. And another prayer to answer.

In addition to his busy life as minister of the Dungannon Church, Trevor conducted some Gospel missions, in other parts of Northern Ireland, as did many of his colleagues.

It was when conducting one such mission in the John Knox Memorial Free Pesbyterian Church, on Belfast's Shankill Road, that something really wonderful happened.

Some years after Trevor's father's death, his wife was remarried. To Roy. And the newly married couple began to attend the Evangelical Presbyterian Church on the Somerton Road. When Trevor heard of this he was thrilled. His mother, who had never shown any inclination towards anything spiritual all her life, was now going regularly to a place where the Gospel was faithfully preached.

Could that possibly be a first step towards an answer to his heartfelt prayers since the day he was saved?

Then, when his mother and Roy moved house to another part of Belfast, they began to attend the services at the John Knox Memorial Free Presbyterian Church. Two things impressed them about Rev. Alan Smylie, minister of that particular church. The first was the clear way in which he presented the Gospel message, and the second was the kindness that he and his wife showed to the new couple in the district.

It was with a special kind of burden, then, that Rev. Trevor Baxter commenced a two-week mission in that church in September, 1993. How he would love to see his mother and stepfather saved!

How diligently and carefully he prepared for those meetings!

How earnestly and fervently he prayed for those meetings!

And Roy and his mother hardly missed a night.

God blessed the preaching of His Word in that mission. Many hearts were challenged. Souls were confronted with the claims of Christ.

On the final Sunday night, when the service was over and almost everyone had left the building, Trevor and Mary were tidying up around the front of the church. Reluctant to get ready to go home. For although there had been blessing at the mission, they felt a peculiar sense of emptiness. They were so disappointed that neither Trevor's mother, or Roy, had come to the Lord.

Perhaps something would happen yet... Surely God had spoken to them... By some word, or text, or even hymn, on at least one of the nights...

Their private ponderings were interrupted by a noise at the back of the building. Suddenly the doors opened and in came Trevor's mother, and Roy, with Rev. and Mrs. Smylie. All four of them walked right up the aisle, in virtual silence, only to disappear again, into the minister's room at the back.

Trevor had been praying that his mother would be saved. And he had done that now every day for the last twenty-seven years. But now, when he saw her going into a room to be counselled, he could hardly take it in! He was thunderstruck! Dumbfounded!

His prayers were being answered before his very eyes! And he wondered if what he had seen was true. Was that really his mother and Roy who had gone through there?

He had to sit down. And keep sitting. His hollow legs began to shake. There was a funny kind of fluttering in his stomach. The colour drained from his face.

It was a totally emotional reaction to a totally marvellous climax to the mission.

When the four of them emerged from the minister's room, about twenty minutes later, and Trevor's mother who was by then over seventy years of age, and Roy, both 'confessed with their mouth the Lord Jesus', everybody wept for joy.

What a wonderful, gracious God they had!

Trevor was so overwhelmed by a sense of spiritual elation after his mum's conversion, that he just couldn't go straight home. There was somebody that he must tell about the tremendous blessing which they had all experienced.

Who else but Dr. Paisley?

And Trevor knew where he could find him, too.

There was to be a communion service held after the main service on that particular evening and he knew that Dr. Paisley would be at the Martyrs Memorial Church for some time yet.

When Trevor and Mary arrived over in the east of the city the communion service was drawing to a close.

However, the overjoyed son couldn't even contain himself to the end. Couldn't wait until the communion was over. This news had to be told! Announced! Broadcast!

He walked quietly up to where Dr. Paisley was seated, sat down beside him, and whispered the wonderful news into his ear.

It wasn't long, either, until he, in turn, passed it on. Announced it to the whole congregation. And another round of rejoicing began!

As Trevor Baxter looks back upon his life there are a number of apparently minor incidents, that turned out to be major milestones, along the way.

He praises God, for example, for the day when he became mesmerised by the outspoken politician on the T.V. news. And also for the day when he bought the three booklets for 'two bob', at the Ballymena rally...

The greatest milestone of all, however, came on the Saturday morning when he accepted Christ as his Saviour and Lord.

For by that one simple act of faith he began a new life in Christ..

Entered upon a new relationship as a child of God..

Started to serve a new Master..

And obtained the title deeds to a new and eternal home in heaven...

'Oh this uttermost salvation,
Tis a fountain full and free,
Pure, exhaustless, ever flowing,
Wondrous grace, it reaches me.'

18

IT'S GOOD TO TALK

❖

D r. Paisley was out at a meeting one evening when the telephone rang at home. His wife answered it.

"Hello, I wonder if I could possibly speak to Dr. Paisley?" a cultured gentleman's voice enquired.

"I'm sorry, he is out at the moment but he will be in later. I am his wife. Could I take a message or help you in any way?" Mrs. Paisley replied.

"I don't know, perhaps you could," the voice went on. "You don't know me, but I will tell you my problem. I am a doctor in England, and just recently I have come to realize that I am not ready to die. And I am afraid of death. I know that what I need is to come to Christ and have my sins washed away. Can you help me with that, or do I need to talk to your husband?"

"Indeed I can help you with that," Eileen Paisley assured him. "Just hold on there a minute until I get my Bible."

When she had found her Bible she opened it, and began to read some relevant Scripture verses to the anxious gentleman at the other end of the line, explaining to him all the while, God's wonderful plan of salvation.

And over the telephone she led the concerned man to Christ.

For months after that happy evening they kept in contact, phoning each other once every two months or so. And always the doctor was rejoicing in the Lord. In the satisfaction and security of his newly-found faith.

Then once when Dr. Paisley and his family were returning from holiday, a thought struck Eileen. "We must give our doctor friend in England a call sometime after we get home, Ian," she suggested. "It seems a long time since we heard from him."

When they had been home a few days, his wife did just that. She called their doctor friend's number.

Surprisingly, it was a lady's voice that answered. When Mrs. Paisley had asked to speak to the doctor, the lady hesitated a moment, then replied, "Obviously you musn't have heard. He died very suddenly a few months ago."

Eileen was stunned.

Their friend was gone.

His worst fears had been realized.

But he had made the correct preparation.

He had been ready.

It was a busy morning in Dr. Paisley's European office on Belfast's Ravenhill Road, when the telephone rang yet again. Mrs. Paisley answered it.

"Hello. Could I speak to Dr. Paisley, please?" a lady asked.

"No, I'm sorry but he is in London at present," Mrs. Paisley told her.

"Well, would his wife be about?" was the next question.

"This is his wife speaking," Eileen replied. "What can I do for you?"

"I have a terrible problem," the caller confided, clearly relieved that she had found somebody whom she thought could help her. "You see, it's like this. My husband was a lovely Christian man, but I was very hard on him because of his beliefs. Gave him 'a lot of stick'. Said all sorts of nasty things to him. Yet he showed real Christian grace. He was really very good to me. Then nearly four months ago he died very suddenly."

She stopped for a moment to recollect her composure. And her thoughts. Mrs. Paisley waited patiently. People like this needed time.

Then the burdened caller continued, "Since he died I have been eaten up by guilt. I can find no peace. The Jehovah's Witnesses have started to call with me, but I know they are not telling the truth. What can I do? How can I get peace and rest in my soul?"

It was a real cry from the heart.

When she was sure that the lady had finished all that she had to say, at least in the meantime, Mrs. Paisley told her gently, "You know the only way that you can have real peace in your soul is to come to your husband's Saviour."

" And how do I do that?" the woman enquired, eagerly. She was pleased that there appeared to be a solution to her problem. A way to rid herself of this millstone of remorse. "Do I have to go up to the front in a church or something?"

"No, indeed," her experienced spiritual advisor assured her. "You can be saved now. Today. There, just where you are."

She then went on to explain to her anxious listener about the love of God, and how that Christ had come to earth to die, to take away her sins. And the guilt of her sins.

Suddenly the caller cried out, "I see it now. I understand it. I believe it."

She was saved.

It had been good to talk to a compassionate counsellor, but it was even better to trust in a loving, sin-cleansing, guilt-removing Saviour.

19

A SOLEMN WARNING

❖

S am Flanagan's grandmother was a Christian, and she liked to check up on her little grandson. Make sure that what he was being taught in school, and Sunday School was to her liking.

As a child, Sam attended Currie Primary School, in Belfast, and a number of different Sunday Schools, and Children's meetings. There he was taught the Bible stories, many of which he was to remember, much later in life. And his granny was always keen to make sure that he knew what they really meant. That they were more than just pleasant little stories about a man called Jesus, who lived long ago.

She told him the Gospel truth.

Explained to him, simply, God's way of salvation.

However, when he came into his teenage years, Sam decided that he was 'grown up', and didn't need to go to Sunday School any more. That kind of thing was 'only for children', he decided. So he left.

Then came the start of 'the Troubles' in Northern Ireland, and this unrest had a profound effect upon the growing lad, by now seventeen. When the situation deteriorated in his area, and the taunts of stone-throwing mobs were replaced by the crack of gunfire, Sam decided that he would have to 'do his bit, for the cause'. So he became involved in paramilitary activity.

This was not unusual for a teenager, living in a staunchly 'loyalist' area at that time. It was what many of the young men did. It was their interest. Their hobby. Their leisure time pursuit.

For the next four years, Sam Flanagan had no time for God. He was too engrossed in what was going on around him. But through those very events, the God whom he had chosen to ignore, made His presence felt. A number of the lads that he had grown up with were killed. A soldier was shot just around the corner from where he lived.

'What would happen if that was me?', he used to ask himself, at such times. And then, shutting it out of his mind, he went on his way again. Until something else occurred to draw him up once more.

After a particularly turbulent period, Sam decided, in 1974, to cut all links with paramilitary organisations, and do something more worthwhile with his life. So he began training as a hairdresser in a city centre salon.

Then, in 1979, Sam Flanagan set up his own hairdressing business. Although he didn't have a lot of experience of management, he knew his work, well. So, after an initial settling-in, word-of-mouth-advertising, period, business at 150 North Queen Street began to prosper.

For the first time in his life, Sam began to taste the sweet flavour of success. He had now money in his pocket, and the freedom to spend it. So he began to indulge in every possible pleasurable activity that he could think of.

I can afford it, so why not try it, became his philosophy.

However, the establishment of his own hairdressing shop had a side-effect that Sam hadn't reckoned upon when he was weighing up the pros and cons of starting his own business.

Christians started to come in to have their hair done. Sam knew many of these local people and respected them. He always had.

As they talked to him, and occasionally to each other, when they happened to be in the shop together, Sam realized that there was something about these people that he didn't have. Many of them, too, told him what the difference was. They were saved. No matter how unsettled things around them became they had a deep settled peace and joy in their souls. And they all appeared to live as they talked as well. They were a contented bunch of individuals.

One of Sam's regular customers was Helen Montgomery. This lady was a Christian who never failed to witness to her faith, given half an opportunity. She often spoke to her hairdresser about spiritual matters, telling him that he would never know real peace or complete fulfilment in life until he was saved.

In addition to witnessing to him, and leaving him little booklets to read, Helen encouraged Sam to go to church. To hear the Gospel.

"Why don't you go over and hear Dr. Paisley in The Martyrs Memorial Church on the Ravenhill Road?" she asked him often. And she wasn't the only one, either. A number of his customers had told him that he should go to hear Dr. Paisley. They had all assured their hairdresser that he would like his style of preaching.

Gradually Sam became more inclined to that idea himself. For two reasons.

Firstly, his parents had a high regard for Dr. Paisley's stand on many issues. He was one public figure who was held in great esteem in the Flannigan household. And Sam would just like to hear what he had to say.

There was an even deeper reason than that, though.

For the last few years, Sam had been earning more and more, and yet had been becoming less and less content. The sense of void and hollow pointlessness in his life was beginning to grow. Instead of enjoyment he had emptiness. There was a vital component missing somewhere. Something that he hadn't discovered yet...

Could it be this salvation that his Christian customers had been telling him about?

It was early in 1986 when Sam Flanagan decided to respond to all the invitations and encouragements. He would go and hear Dr. Paisley preaching in the Martyrs Memorial Church.

So, on Sunday 26th January he went along, joining the large crowd at the evening service.

The singing was impressive. And the preaching was powerful.

As Dr. Paisley proclaimed the Gospel, clearly, the Holy Spirit began to work on Sam's soul. Salvation, he realized, was what he was craving, to give him the satisfaction in life that he had been seeking for so long. He needed to come to Christ. Have his sins forgiven.

At the close of the service, Dr. Paisley made his appeal. "As our heads are bowed, and our eyes are closed, and the people of God are praying...don't hesitate to come to the Saviour. He is calling you. Now. Here. Tonight.."

When he invited anyone interested to 'come up and speak to me. I will be in the room at the back here,' Sam determined that he was going to talk to the preacher.

He wanted to be right with God. And he longed for the joy of sins forgiven.

As others filed out at the front of the church, he waited until the way was clear, and then walked up and out to the back.

When someone had directed him to Dr. Paisley's room, Sam found it, went in respectfully, and found the speaker there.

"I would like to speak to you, sir," he began.

Not recognising the man before him, and reckoning that he could only have made his way in there for one important purpose, Dr. Paisley asked him directly, "Do you want to be saved?"

"I do," Sam replied, briefly. Honestly.

"Well, come on in then and we will have a talk," the preacher invited.

After Sam had sat down, Dr. Paisley began to read a series of verses from the Bible to him. A few of them he remembered from his childhood days, but most were unfamiliar. As he read the texts, in a significant sequence, Dr. Paisley showed Sam how he could have his sins forgiven by trusting in the work of Christ at Calvary.

When he had finished his explanation, Dr. Paisley closed his Bible, and he and Sam knelt down, side by side. The spiritual counsellor prayed first, and then Sam cried out, in prayer, "Lord have mercy on me, and save me."

There and then, God heard his cry. And answered his plea from the heart.

The Lord had mercy on him.

Sam Flanagan was saved.

When he arrived home and told his mother that he had come to Jesus, she appeared pleased. Said that it was 'nice'. But then went on to let him know that although 'religion' might be all right for him, it wasn't for her.

Now Sam had something to live for. At last there was some sense of purpose to his existence. So he began to witness to others. Tell them about what God had done for him.

He was particularly concerned about the friends with whom he used to spend every weekend. 'Enjoying himself.' He told them all of the joy which salvation had brought into his barren life. And invited them to come to church with him.

Although some of his once-upon-a-time-mates made fun of his stance as a Christian, and the very thought of going to church was 'a real laugh', two of his friends, in particular, appeared interested.

One of them, Philip, promised Sam that he would go along to church with him. Sometime. In fact, he confessed, but made Sam promise not to tell 'the others', that he had met a Christian girl in the city centre once. After an open-air service. This girl was now writing to him, sending him Gospel literature, and pointing out his need of salvation.

Then there was Roy, who also assured Sam that he would go to church with him. Sometime. All that was holding him back, he said, was that he had 'nothing decent to wear'.

"My mother likes the thought of me going to a church," he maintained. "And she says she is going to buy me a suit. When she does that I will go to church with you."

Then, exactly five weeks after his conversion, on Sunday 2nd March, Sam heard dreadful, shocking news.

His two friends, who were both going to come to hear the Gospel, sometime, had been out with some others, in Bangor, Co. Down on the previous night. On their way home to Belfast, in the early hours of that Sunday morning, the car in which they had been travelling was involved in a road traffic accident.

And they were both killed.

Neither of them had ever come to church. Or to Christ.

The sudden and tragic deaths of his two friends had an immediate and intense effect upon the new Christian.

They came as a solemn warning to him. A painful lesson.

They emphasised for him that time was short.

Death was sure.

Witnessing was important.

Whilst continuing in his work as a hairdresser, Sam began to become increasingly more involved in other activities, totally unrelated to shampoos, scissors, and blasts of hot air. He kept a stock of Gospel tracts in his shop. And should a customer show any inclination to discuss spiritual matters, he gave them a suitable tract before they left.

When away from 150, North Queen Street, Sam commenced teaching in the Sunday School at Martyrs Memorial Free Presbyterian Church, and helping with door-to-door evangelism. He so much relished the opportunity to tell others, whether young or old, of what God had done for him And could do for others. It was so rewarding.

In 1989, the hairdresser felt that God was calling him to give up his hairdressing, and go to Bible College to train for full-time Christian work in some capacity.

The part of him which had become so accustomed to a pleasant, money-to-spend lifestyle, seemed to counter such aspirations. "You would be silly to give up such a profitable business," it seemed to insist.

For more than a year, Sam struggled with it.

Should he? Or shouldn't he?

Then one day, while he was turning the matter over in his mind, as he often did, a verse came to him. One he had heard or learnt somewhere, long before. It impressed itself forcibly and constantly on his thoughts.

It was 1 Timothy 6 v 6. 'Godliness with contentment is great gain'.

It was the phrase, 'great gain' that arrested him. He wouldn't be losing anything to pursue 'godliness'. In fact a huge and lasting profit was promised. Great gain.

So, in 1990, Sam sold his hairdressing business, and enrolled in the Whitefield College of The Bible, where he studied for a number of years.

Since then, Sam Flanagan has been engaged in full-time Christian work, and at the present time is conducting Bible Studies in the Shankill Road area of Belfast, and praying that God will open the door to further opportunities of service for him.

20

WELL, THAT'S IT!

❖

It was autumn, 1997. Mrs. Paisley sat alone at the back of an auction-room in Banbridge, Co. Down. Truth to tell, she hadn't really planned to be there at all. There were so many things waiting to be attended to at home. But her husband had encouraged her to go.

"Come with me, Eileen, for the company," he had urged. "You can sit at the back and watch the goings-on. And you never know, there could just be some things there that I might be interested in. I may need your advice."

As she sat there, casually observing the busy, and occasionally noisy, proceedings, a young man ambled into the auction-room. He came over to where Mrs. Paisley sat, and began to talk. First about the weather, then about the auction. When they had been talking for a few minutes and the auction-watching-wife had explained why she was there, and who she was with, the stranger said, rather to her surprise, "I didn't see you in Strasbourg with your husband".

"I suppose that is because I wasn't there," she replied with a smile. She had been on a number of European trips. But none recently.

The chap then told her how he had come to be in Strasbourg.

"I first met your husband at the Balmoral Show last year," he explained, "and he said he would pray for me." He went on to say that he had joined the DUP and when he heard of a trip to Europe he decided to go along. "When I was there, with that party, I met some people who were Christians. They were extremely friendly and made me feel very welcome. But they also witnessed to me. Telling me that I needed to be saved..."

Not quite sure whether he had more to tell or not, Mrs. Paisley interrupted him, briefly. "Well, if he said that he would pray for you, then you can take it from me that he has been doing it," she assured him, confidently.

She knew him better that most!

The young man then said, quite earnestly, "I would really love to be saved."

"You could be saved, just there where you are, you know," Mrs. Paisley replied, simply, looking across at him.

The sincere seeker appeared rather puzzled. That was news to him. "You mean I don't have to put up my hand, or walk out at the front of one of your churches or anything like that?" he enquired, quizzically.

"No. All you need to do is come in simple faith to the Saviour," she went on. "And you could do that right here."

Just with that Dr. Paisley joined the pair of them. He had come back to speak to his wife. Seeking the kind of advice that he had encouraged her to come to the auction to give, if required. Her opinion on something that he had contemplated buying.

When she had spoken to him about his possible purchase, she had a request to make of her husband.

"Ian, could you lend me your New Testament for a few minutes?" she asked him.

Dr. Paisley handed over the little pocket Testament which he always carried with him, spoke to the young man, whom he recognised, and left them to continue their conversation.

As she leafed through the Testament to find appropriate verses, Mrs. Paisley said to the young man, "Let me read to you something of what the Bible says about how you can be saved." And when she began to read out some of the texts which she had chosen, she was amazed to discover that her listener could finish off quite a number of them. Obviously he knew somthing of the Word of God. That could only be helpful.

When she had finished reading and explaining God's plan of salvation for 'the whosoever will', she thought it would be best to challenge him directly.

"Do you really want to be saved?" she asked.

"Yes, indeed I do," he replied. Nothing that he had heard had in any way influenced him to change his mind. In fact, just the opposite was the case. It had only served to strengthen his resolve.

"Well then, why not just trust in the Lord, where you are sitting there?" she encouraged.

And the young man from Co. Tyrone did just as she had suggested. Bowing his head, silently, oblivious to all the hubbub around him, he consciously accepted the Lord Jesus into his heart.

When he had done so he looked across at the woman who had so patiently led him to the foot of the cross, and remarked, happily, emphatically, "Well, that's it!"

"Yes," his counsellor echoed his words, "that's it! The transaction is complete. You are now saved. God has made you His child by faith."

The new believer's face was radiant. He looked so very happy. But his immediate concern was for someone else.

"Now I would love to see my mother saved," he said.

"Well then, we will all start praying for her now," Mrs. Paisley promised him.

When she saw him, again, two months after his auction-room confession of Christ as Saviour, he exclaimed enthusiastically, "I never thought that being saved could bring me such peace and such joy!"

There are two days in his life which that young man will never forget.

The day when he first made personal contact with Dr. Paisley at Balmoral Show.

And infinitely more importantly, the day when he made a personal commitment to the Lord Jesus Christ at a Banbridge auction.

21

THIS MARRIAGE NEEDS
A MIRACLE

❖

As a ten-year old boy, Hugh Robert Thompson crawled around the floor after his father. They were nailing down the floor boards of the new Free Presbyterian Church in Portavogie. Joe Thompson drove the nails half-way in, and son Hugh Robert followed him round to hammer them home. It made him feel big. Important. Useful. Grown-up.

Hugh Robert had been going along to meetings since early childhood. He heard ministers like John Douglas, John Wylie, Cecil Menary, and on the odd very special occasion, Ian Paisley, preach on Sunday evenings in Ballyhalbert Orange Hall. So encouraging had the response been to those early meetings that it was decided to establish a Free Presbyterian Church in the Co. Down fishing village of Portavogie. And young Hugh Robert played his part in the completion of that building. Helping to nail down the floorboards.

During his teenage years Hugh Robert attended that church most Sundays, to hear Rev. John Douglas preach. His parents, Joe and Ruby Thompson, were dedicated Christians, and went along to church at every possible opportunity. It was their main interest in life. Their son went along with them on Sundays. Sometimes willingly. Sometimes not just so willingly. But he went. And he heard the Gospel.

Then when he was eighteen years of age, two things happened in the life of Hugh Robert Thompson, both of which were to lead to a rapid deterioration in any little inclination that he had towards spiritual matters.

The first was that he was persuaded by a mate to try a glass of home-brewed beer. Although he knew that his parents wouldn't approve, for he had never seen alcoholic drink in his house in his life, the young man succumbed to the temptation. He didn't want to appear 'chicken'. Wanted to prove that he was as good a man as any of them.

Although he only had slightly more than a pint of that home-made brew, Hugh Robert's companions had to walk him around the shore for nearly two hours until he sobered up sufficiently to go home.

But Hugh Robert Thompson was hooked. On alcohol.

It was at this time also that he went to sea on a fishing trawler. Although the life at sea could often be tough the pay was good. And it was the traditional occupation of so many of the men in Portavogie. Some of these boats left the Co. Down port on a Monday morning and only returned once in midweek to land a catch before coming into harbour on Friday evening for the weekend. All the other nights were spent put into ports like Peel and Ramsey on the Isle of Man, or Campbeltown on the Mull of Kintyre.

Life on board a fishing trawler was simple. Often rough. Always repetitive. The boat left port at five or six in the morning and the crew fished all day. Then in the evening, when the day's work was done and the trawler was safely tied up in a harbour, the 'drinking-men' washed, changed and headed ashore. Straight into the nearest public house. The skippers, the Christians, and indeed all the quieter crew members, stayed on board. In the early hours of the morning the 'revellers' staggered, or were carried, back to their vessel and fell asleep in their bunk in a drunken stupor, only to be awakened by the throb of the engines on the way to the fishing grounds.When it was time to start fishing the men-with-the-hangover from the night before were ready to start work. What was left of the day, spent in the brisk sea-air, revived everybody sufficiently to allow them to do their job. And to be ready for the next night...

Away from home, away from his parents' godly influence, with money in his pocket and the desire to 'have a good time' in his heart, young Hugh Robert Thompson soon fitted into that pattern. It became his way of life. He soon became addicted to drink.

When he was twenty-one, Hugh Robert was married.

And when the was twenty-four, his marriage failed.

But he didn't care. All that Hugh Robert Thompson wanted to do was fish all day and drink all night and right over the weekend. Every penny that he earned was spent in a public house somewhere. He had become a slave to alcohol.

Meantime, Joe and Ruby, his parents, were breaking their hearts over him. Their concern for their headstrong, wayward son became a terrible burden. How they loved him! How they pleaded with God, in prayer, for him.

Occasionally, they would see little chinks of light in the gloom. Rays of hope. Distant rainbows. For Hugh Robert respected his parents and what they believed. He tried never to turn up at their house drunk. And every once in a while he would go to Church with them on a Sunday evening. Especially if he heard that Dr. Paisley was speaking. There was something about his style of preaching that fascinated the by-now-hardened fisherman.

Hugh Robert sat glued to his seat, a number of times, in his twenties, as Dr. Paisley solemnly proclaimed the Gospel message. He knew that he should respond, give his life to Christ, but he wasn't prepared to give up the drink. And then there were his companions. What would they say?

No. He decided that he wasn't going to have anything to do with God. Or salvation. Or Christianity. So he blocked out the appeal. Thought about other things. Planned the week ahead. Just refused to listen, in case he would be 'caught'.

His parents, however, continued to pray constantly that he would be preserved. And saved.

It was during the summer of 1980 that Kathleen Bunting spied Hugh Robert Thompson on Portavogie harbour. Kathleen was doing some part-time work to earn a few extra pounds for a holiday, when she became attracted to the hard-working hard-drinking fisherman.

When she told her friends how she 'fancied' him, how she would like to meet him, 'go out with him', even, they all warned her off.

H.R.Thompson was 'bad news'.

Everybody knew that, they said.

All he was interested in was himself and the booze, they advised.

Did you not know that he has already had a broken marriage? they enquired.

She was not for turning, though, and Kathleen struck up a conversation with him one day. And they hadn't been chatting too long, or too often, until Hugh Robert found something appealing about this younger woman.

They began to see each other more often, and during those days of courtship Hugh Robert seemed to pay fewer visits to the pubs. He realized that he loved 'Kate', as he chose to call her, and she in turn believed that if they were married she could have a settling influence on him. Help him to change his ways.

Against the advice of many who knew him, including his own father, who warned Kate, from bitter experience, that 'Hugh Robert will break your heart', the couple were engaged in July, 1984, and married on 7th December, in that same year.

Sadly, things didn't turn out as Kate had hoped. She didn't prove herself able to influence her husband. For although Hugh Robert had stopped going to sea as a fisherman, he took over his father's business as a fish merchant, travelling across north Down and into Belfast, selling fish into shops. This afforded him ample opportunity to spend the day's, or half the week's, takings, in a pub on the way home.

There were many times when someone would telephone either Kate or her in-laws to tell them that Hugh Robert's van was parked in

Kircubbin. And that he was in a public house. Full drunk. Then Joe Thompson had to set out to bring his son, and his van, home to Portavogie. Distressing for a Christian father. And equally distressing for a young wife, who was also, by now, a mother.

The birth of baby Kyle, instead of bringing lasting joy and stability to the young parents, only added more tension to an already stress-stretched-to-the-limit relationship. For in addition to caring for their baby son, Kate was endeavouring to 'keep the books' for the business. But this proved to be an almost impossible task, for so much of their possible income was spent on liquor that it never made it to the house. Not to mention the books.

And when Kate tried to discuss their problems, and suggest solutions, she was totally ignored. So much so that she began to concentrate on rearing her little son, and ignoring her husband..

It eventually came to the stage that meaningful communication between the couple broke down completely. The weekends were 'all picture and no sound'.

To escape the sullen silence that was supposed to be 'home', on a Friday or Saturday night, Hugh Robert went out in his van. Alone. Then, about midnight, if he hadn't returned, Kate phoned the Pigeon Club in Portavogie, and around all the pubs in the neighbouring villages. To try and locate her husband

If he happened to be still in Portavogie, she lifted their baby from his cot, wrapped him in his snowsuit, and set out, walking, with little Kyle in the buggy, to retrieve the keys of the van from her inebriated spouse. She was so scared that he would try to drive home, drunk. And kill somebody.

If, however, he was in a neighbouring village, she was forced to enlist the help of her husband's long-suffering yet brokenhearted parents, who were a tremendous support to their young, struggling daughter-in-law, in many different ways.

One of the most important things that Joe and Ruby Thompson did for Kate, was to encourage her to come with them to the Sunday evening Gospel sevice in Portavogie Free Presbyterian Church. And the young mother loved to go. The people were friendly and sympathetic. And the message was a complete revelation to her. Although she had attended church in her earlier days, she had never heard the Gospel. She had no idea that she needed to be saved. So she used to sit in those services and long to come to Christ. Then she put it off. "Have I not enough problems in my life at the minute without having to live a good life?" she reasoned with herself. "How could I ever do that in my situation?"

On Good Friday, 1989, Hugh Robert had calls to make in Belfast. Fresh fish to deliver to a number of retail outlets. Beside many of these fish-and-chip shops there was a handy public house. So he called in for a drink. Just 'a wee one'. However, by the time he arrived in Portavogie, in the late afternoon, he was barely capable of being in charge of a vehicle. But even then he didn't go home. He went to the Pigeon Club. To round off the day.

When he staggered home to his house, having left the van behind, Hugh Robert knew that Kate and the children would be in bed. So he wouldn't disturb them. He went into the garage, to climb up into the loft where he had made himself a makeshift bed. For sleeping off the drink.

About 11.30, Kate thought she heard a noise. Moaning and groaning. Coming from the garage. So she took a torch and went out. It was, as she expected, her husband. Lying in a heap. Groaning on the floor. She had seen him like that before, many a time. So she thought nothing of it. Threw a blanket over him. And closed down the garage door. Went back into the house, and went back to bed. He would be O.K. in the morning. He always was.

About 1.00 a.m. Kate was awakened by a commotion outside. Joe and Ruby Thompson, and an ambulance, had arrived. A neighbour had phoned for them when he heard a noise in the garage, went to investigate, and found that there appeared to be more the matter with Hugh Robert than his usual drunken insensibility. He was by then yelling out in pain.

Hugh Robert had fallen from the loft on to the garage floor. And had, as it turned out, broken his leg.

Kate was overwhelmed by guilt. But what was she to do? Her patience with her husband was fast running out.

When Hugh Robert was discharged from hospital, sober, on crutches, and with his leg in plaster, he maintained that he would never drink again.

"That has been a painful lesson to me. That is the end of it now," he vowed.

Kate listened to him, without reply. She found it rather hard to believe. Had she not heard all that kind of stuff before? Dozens of times?

And she was right to be sceptical, too.

For it wasn't very long until her husband arived home again, drunk, one night. On the crutches.

The most difficult time in their married lives came in June, 1990. Kate was expecting their third child, and Hugh Robert was still up to his old tricks.

On Monday, 25th, there was a fish sale in Kilkeel at 4.00 p.m. Hugh Robert told his wife, though, that the sale was at 2.00 p.m. That would give him a couple of hours for a round of the pubs before it started.

Hugh Robert made it to the pubs. But he didn't make it to the sale. Never saw a fish. Never mind buying any.

About 4.00 p.m. Kate had a telephone call. From a bar in Kilkeel. It was her husband. Semi-drunk. She put the phone down, in disgust.

Then she bethought herself. What happens if he tries to drive home from there and kills somebody on the road?

She phoned the public house in Kilkeel where she reckoned he was most likely to be. To tell them to take the car keys from him. She would send somebody to bring him home. But it was too late. They told her that he wasn't there.

Kate panicked. She phoned her in-laws, in desperation. They were so kind. So supportive.

When they came to her aid, Joe set out, with a driver, for Kilkeel, to try and find his wayward son, and Ruby stayed with Kate and the two young children.

As the the heat of a summer day gave way to the welcome cool of a summer evening the two women sat waiting for news. Kate occasionally burst into tears.

"This marriage needs a miracle," she sobbed. "It can't go on like this much longer. I have just had enough!"

Her mother-in-law understood her. Perfectly. Had Joe not warned her what would happen, years before?

Meanwhile, back in Kilkeel, Hugh Robert Thompson, who could hardly stand, decided to return to Portavogie. Driving himself.

But he only made it as far as Newcastle. Fourteen miles down the road. Someone had reported a car being driven dangerously, and the police caught up with him, and stopped him, at a large roundabout on the outskirts of the Co. Down holiday resort.

When they opened the driver's door of the car, the fish merchant with no fish fell out at their feet.

He was brought to the local Police station, where blood samples were taken. And he was detained for a while. For questioning.

Later, the policemen took him down to a restaurant in the town, telling him to have something to eat and then return to the station. Hugh Robert waited until they, and their car, were safely out of sight, then walked out of the restaurant. Straight into the pub, a few doors up.

When Joe Thompson was passing Newcastle Police Station, he spotted his son's car parked outside it. Not a hopeful sign.

He went into the station, identified himself, and was informed that his son was 'up in the town for something to eat'. So he set out again to search, with a heavy heart.

Hugh Robert was now in big trouble. That was obvious.

The concerned father didn't have to search long for his unconcerned son, however. As they drove back towards the town centre Joe and the driver saw him. Zig-zagging unsteadily along South Promenade. Towards the Police Station.

After assuring the Police that he would untertake to see his son safely home, Joe Thompson brought Hugh Robert back to Portavogie to the two anxiously waiting, sometimes weeping, women. And the driver brought home his car.

As a result of that episode, Hugh Robert was later fined one hundred pounds, and lost his licence for a year.

After Joe and Ruby had left later that evening, not happy, but at least glad that their son and daughter-in-law were both under the same roof, Hugh Robert and Kate retired, speechlessly, to bed.

But the crisis wasn't over yet. There was more.

As morning approached Kate wakened her husband. She had to speak to him now. And urgently.

"Hugh Robert, you are going to have to get me to Ards Hospital as soon as you can. I think I am going to lose the baby,"she shouted at him. Stirring him into sensible action.

When they had made arrangements for Kyle and Scott, their existing family, Hugh Robert and Kate drove to the Hospital in Newtownards. But it was too late. And fruitless. At ten o'clock on Tuesday morning, Kate had a miscarriage.

As Hugh Robert Thompson stood trembling beside his wife's bed in Ards Hospital, Kate was weeping her heart out . Again.

"God is punishing the both of us because of you. We have lost our baby!" she sobbed.

Her husband shivered. Quivered. Uncontrollably. Like a leaf on a tree. No matter how hard he tried, he just couldn't stop himself shaking.

"Things will be different from now on, Kate," he pledged for the umpteenth time. "You'll see."

He was right enough about that. She would 'see'.

Did he really mean it? Had he learnt his lesson at last? How could she ever believe him?

In August, the Thompson family went to Scotland for a holiday. In a caravan. At the start of their fortnight, this proved to be a bit of a test for Hugh Robert. The nearest pub was in a village nearly three miles away. And Kate insisted on keeping the keys of the car. "I can't leave the boys here in the caravan to go looking for you in the middle of the night." she told him.

He would just have to try and do without.

Amazingly, he found that easier to do than he had ever expected. For something was happening in his life. Something which, at the time, he didn't even understand.

God was beginning to answer his parents' passionate prayers for their problem son.

There was a Bible in that caravan.

And The Gulf War was looming up.

In the evenings, when their two little boys were safely tucked up in their bunks, sound asleep, Hugh Robert and Kate began to talk together. Happily. Sensibly. Gladly.

They became preoccupied with world events. What was going to happen? How was it all going to finish? What, or when, would be 'the end of the world'?

Prophecy. This was something that Kate had never heard of before. Knew nothing about. But Hugh Robert did. He had heard preaching about it in his youth.

Kate was fascinated to be told by her husband that the answer to many of their questions would be in the Bible. So they started to read the one in the caravan. And spend time discussing it together.

Hugh Robert was convicted by their conversations. There he was, a virtually good-for-nothing husband, explaining to his seemingly endlessly patient wife, about prophecy! How ironic!

Secretly, he would love to be saved. He knew fine well that he wasn't ready to meet God. But what about the drink? How could he ever give it up?

When they returned from holiday, they both went to a meeting in Donaghadee Community Centre. To hear Dr. Paisley preaching.

In the course of his address, the speaker made the remark, "There are hearts here, in this room, that have turned to stone."

Now it was Kate's turn to be challenged. Could that possibly be me? she wondered. Or is it Hugh Robert? Or both of us?

God had begun to work in both of their hearts, independently. Gently nudging them to think about Him.

In the afternoon of Sunday, 9th September, 1990, an anniversary service was held in Portavogie Free Presbyterian Church.

Hugh Robert and Kate went along to that service with Joe and Ruby. They all loved to hear Dr. Paisley preaching. There was something unique about his presentation. His grasp of the Scriptures, and fearless declaration of the truth, appealed to them.

The jam-packed service began formally. Like any other ordinary meeting. Dr. Paisley read from Hebrews chapter 12. And began to speak on the theme of 'Looking unto Jesus'. The message was both plain and powerful.

Then, about fifteen minutes before the service was due to end, something happened. Something unusual. Dramatic. Something that could only be described as a movement of God.

A young woman, sitting near the back of the church, cried out. Aloud. In anguish. She wanted to be saved.

After that, some words which Dr. Paisley quoted struck right to the core of Kate's heart and conscience. They were from the Gospels. Words of Jesus. Matthew 23 v 37. 'O Jerusalem, Jerusalem, thou that killest the prophets, and stonest them which are sent unto thee, how often would I have gathered thy children together, even as a hen gathereth her chickens under her wings, and ye would not!"

She felt that was her. God had called her often. In meetings. At home. In that holiday caravan. But she had done nothing about it. Made no response. She 'would not.'

Sitting there in that church, between her husband and her mother-in-law, Kate Thompson trusted in Christ as her Saviour. She came to Him in a simple act of faith. Responded to the call. At last.

Then she could hardly wait for the appeal at the end. She felt like standing up and yelling, "I've got saved!" But she didn't. She restrained herself. With some difficulty.

Kate was sure that Dr. Paisley would make an appeal at the close of that service. She had heard him make appeals in less Spirit-saturated situations than this. Something special, something wonderful, was happening here.

Sure enough, as he brought his message to an end, Dr. Paisley began to appeal for souls to come to the Saviour.

"I believe that God is at work in this church in a mighty way, today," he announced, obviously sensing the pervading presence of God, himself. "So now we are going to pray. And as our heads are bowed and our eyes are closed, if you feel that God has been speaking to you, and you would like to be saved, just put up your hand and we will see you. And speak to you about God's wonderful way of salvation..."

Kate didn't need to hear that appeal a second time!

She had forgotten about her husband .

She had forgotten about her family.

She had forgotten about her troubled marriage.

But she had received Christ!

And what was more, she wanted everybody to know!

At first she raised her hand timidly, up to shoulder level. Then, growing bolder, and afraid, perhaps, that the preacher wouldn't see it, she stuck it straight up in the air, and waved it all around!

Every single person in that service was going to know what God had done in her heart!

When the further invitation was given, a few minutes later, for all those interested to come forward for counselling, Kate was one of the first up the aisle. Although she had already come to the Lord, she wanted everybody to know. So she left Hugh Robert sitting with his parents, who were both in tears. She was determined to make a public confession of her faith. 'Stand up and be counted' for Jesus.

The atmosphere in that church that afternoon had become almost electric. So intense. Charged with a sense of the power of God. People were weeping openly. Unashamedly. Kate glanced up at the platform. The local minister, Rev. David Park, appeared stunned. As if he were glued to the wall behind him. He just couldn't believe what was happening.

Kate was escorted, with others, into the minister's room at the front of the church. For counselling. Samuel Beattie, one of the church elders, read to her from Isaiah chapter 53, and began to tell her of God's way of salvation. But Kate was already saved. Samuel's Scripture reading and explanation merely served to confirm that for her.

Meanwhile, Dr. Paisley was trying to bring the service to a close. The doxology was sung. Then he made his way down to the door to shake hands with the people as they left. But hardly anybody moved. Only a few went out. The greater majority of the congregation remained behind.

Some were praying. Most were weeping. God was working.

Hugh Robert Thompson hadn't budged. Not an inch. He remained fixed to his seat. In turmoil. He knew he should be saved. He knew that this was the right time to be saved. But he was afraid. Scared stiff. Something kept telling him that he couldn't do without the drink. He was just going to let himself down, again. Yet another time.

But Kate was away. Through the door out at the front. Gone to get saved, he was sure. She certainly looked as though she meant business. What should he do?...

Dr. Paisley came back into the church. And began praying in the aisle. When he had finished, someone told him about Hugh Robert, who was still sitting in his seat. With a war going on in his soul.

The big preacher came down beside him, and placed a hand gently on his shoulder. "Do you not think it is about time you were saved?" he asked.

Tears streamed down the habitual drinker's face. He had begun to shake again. Visibly. Uncontrollably. Like he had done in the hospital.

"I think it is," he whispered.

"Come on out with me then, and we will have a talk about it," Dr. Paisley invited.

Hugh Robert rose and followed him, with bowed head, out into a room at the back of the church.

In that room Dr. Paisley read some Scripture portions to Hugh Robert, who was by that time so broken that he didn't hear a single word that the preacher read. Or said. Then the experienced preacher and counsellor put his arm around the distraught man's shoulder, and prayed for him. And as he did that Hugh Robert Thompson trusted Christ as his personal Saviour.

While her husband was in the room at the back with Dr. Paisley, Kate emerged from the room at the front. Her face, where it wasn't smudged with tears, was shining with joy.

Her mother-in-law rushed over and hugged her. And hugged her. "Kate, you have got your miracle!" she exclaimed. "You have got your miracle!"

Then, when Hugh Robert came back to join them, Kate and her husband looked at each other in loving astonishment. Beautiful bewilderment. Tender surprise. God had done something wonderful in each of their lives. They were now united in a most marvellous manner. In Christ.

And still nobody moved out of the church!

Nobody wanted to be the first to move out of that atmosphere. It was so unique. It would have been, they felt, like consciously and carelessly moving out of the immediate presence of God Himself.

So they stayed. Sobbing. Praying. Praising God.

Eventually, though, after a prolonged period of rejoicing, they all went home.

And how things had changed in the Thompson household!

Kate could hardly believe it! She was so happy.

Hugh Robert could hardly believe it! He was so happy.

Both of them realized that they had never really lived until that wonderful afternoon when they both came to know the Saviour. Now they were experiencing what Jesus had spoken about. Having, and living, 'life...more abundantly'.

Hugh Robert's drinking companions shook their heads when they heard the news of their former mate's conversion. "He will never be able to do without a drink," they forecast. "He will be back on the bottle in a month."

But he wasn't. Not in one month. Or two. Or three. Or twelve.

Two years after they were saved, one of Hugh Robert's erstwhile drinking pals called at the door one night. And was invited in.

Kate made him a cup of tea, and he sat looking across the kitchen table at she and her husband, his gaze flitting back and forth from one contented face to the other. After a few minutes of such contemplation, he remarked, seriously, "I just wish that I had what you people have. This is a different home from mine, I can tell you!"

It was, indeed, a different home from his.

And it was also a different home from the one it used to be.

The marriage that needed 'a miracle' had been provided with one.

By the grace and mercy of God.

22

HAPPY WITH THE HOLD-UP

❖

The delay was frustrating. Dr. Paisley and his wife Eileen had been very busy on their trip to America and they were so much looking forward to getting home again. To the busy round of church, work and family commitments. But the announcement had just been made... The Virgin Atlantic flight to London would be delayed for one hour.

Annoying, but there was nothing they could do but make the best of it.

Then came a second announcement. As the flight to London would be further delayed all passengers booked on that flight would be taken to a local hotel where a buffet meal would be provided.

That at least would be something.

As the two trying-to-be-patient travellers sat at a table waiting to be called for their meal, a well-dressed lady in her thirties joined them.

After they had exchanged the usual muted moans about the delay, and the problems of travelling in general, Dr. Paisley and his wife gathered that this new acquaintance was something of a seasoned traveller.

Then she told them her story.

Her husband had come over from England and had set himself up in business in U.S.A. Things had gone well for him, and now they had two houses. One in England. One in America.

The lady had a big problem. Her husband expected her to be with him in America every other week, and yet she had a guilty conscience about being so far away from the children who were at a boarding school in Britain. She felt they were being sacrificed on the altar of success. Yet she also wanted to spend as much time with her husband as she possibly could. In order to save their marriage.

After a few minutes spent outlining her dilemma she ended with a sigh, and the pathetic observation, " I just feel as though I am being torn apart. Yet I have nobody. I mean nobody to turn to. To talk to."

Feeling sorry for the lady, and yet pleased that she had confided in them, Dr. Paisley looked at her, and said, gently, "You could talk to the Lord, you know. Eileen and I talk to Him about all sorts of things. Our family, our friends. All our cares and concerns. As a matter of fact everything. We bring everything to the Lord in prayer."

Having paused a minute to let that sink in, he went on, "Tell us this, do you know the Lord ?"

The lady was taken aback. Puzzled. "Well, I read the Bible now and again, but I never found it much of a help, for I don't really understand what it is all about," she confessed. "And sometimes I try to pray. But that doesn't seem to do much good either."

Recognising that confused lady to be a seeking, searching soul, Dr. Paisley produced his Bible and read a number of different verses. After he had explained to her about sin and salvation, about the love of God and the death of Christ on Calvary for her sin, and His call to her to come unto Him, that lady, sitting at a hotel dining-table, simply trusted in Christ for salvation.

And immediately found a Friend whom she could talk to about anything. Anywhere. And at any time.

When it was announced that the meal was now ready, Dr. Paisley stood up. Turning to his wife, he said, "You just sit there and talk to the lady, Eileen. I will go up and get us all something to eat."

With that he strode off.

When the two women were left alone, the new convert gazed at Mrs. Paisley and said, with a contented smile, "Oh, I am really glad that plane was delayed. I honestly felt that my life was falling apart. And now since I have met you and your husband, and come to know the Lord, I feel a whole new sense of peace. Life should certainly be more meaningful from now on."

It has been, too. She has lived to prove it.

23

A DIFFERENT SET OF
GOAL POSTS

❖

Jim and Helen Bailie loved the Lord. And they also loved their three children, Colin, Stuart and Debra. They prayed for them daily and took them to church and sent them to Sunday School. As concerned Christian parents, their overriding ambition for their family was that they should each come to know Christ as Saviour.

The Bailie family lived in Dundonald on the outskirts of Belfast, and attended Newtownards Congregational Church where they sat under the faithful ministry of Pastor Clive Moore.

It was his early experiences at Brooklands Gospel Hall Sunday School, though, that made a lasting impression on Colin, the eldest of the family. The Sunday School was crammed with children from the village and the nearby Ballybeen estate.

Colin was taught for a number of years in that Sunday School by John Brown. This John was a big but gentle gentleman. And the children in his classes liked him. For two reasons. He was not only kind and caring in his approach to them, but he was also 'a sort of famous', too. For after all, didn't he sing in the Templemore Male Choir? He even had his picture on the sleeve of a long-playing record that Colin's parents had in the house!

John, along with many of the other teachers in that Sunday School, encouraged the children to learn long passages from the Bible off by heart. A worthwhile exercise, as it was to turn out.

Colin was the only one from his class at Primary School to go on to a Grammar School, but for him that was not a happy experience. He languished for three years at Grosvenor High School, not because the teaching wasn't good, for it was, but because he wasn't able to play competitive football there. In those early teenage years playing football had become the absorbing passion of his life.

During the three years when Colin was at 'Grosvenor' the Bailie family changed churches. They began to attend Sandown Free Presbyterian Church. Colin was taken along there every Sunday to hear Rev. David Mc Ilveen earnestly preaching the Gospel. He knew the message, for he had heard it so often. He was well aware of the fact that if he was ever going to be in heaven, he needed to be saved.

Although Colin knew the truth of the Gospel, doing anything about it didn't figure at all in his plan for life ahead. The dream of becoming a successful professional footballer dominated the thinking time of all his waking hours. He could just see the contract forms..hear the roar of a fifty-thousand-or-so crowd... feel the spring of the famous Wembley turf beneath his expensive sponsored boots...finger the big fat roll of ten-pound notes in his pocket...

And all that didn't leave a lot of time for God.

Anyway, the Devil kept pumping him with the fallacy that he couldn't be a Christian AND a big-time professional footballer.

So, he literally dispelled all thoughts of salvation from his mind. They were going to get in his way, and nothing at all could be allowed to do that. Nothing. The major thing for him, the important thing, indeed the only thing, was to go 'across the water', and play for a big-name football club.

When Colin was fourteen years of age two things happened in his life that were important rungs in his climb up the ladder to footballing success.

Firstly, he changed schools. From 'Grosvenor' to Dundonald Boys High School. The curriculum at Dundonald wasn't quite as academic as it had been at the former school. It was more vocational. Not that Colin cared a tuppenny-ticket about curriculums. He could play football at Dundonald. And that was all that mattered!

Colin's footballing aspirations were given a tremendous boost when he joined Dungoyne Boy's Club, which was based on the Ballybeen estate. It didn't take the leaders of that Club, Jack Mc Kittrick, Jim Waring, and Roy Allen, long to realise that this 'new boy' had an exceptional footballing talent. And they were prepared to push him. As far as the lad could go. The lad himself didn't that mind either!

So successful were the leaders of that Boy's Club in their promotion of Colin, that when he was only fifteen years of age Colin Bailie travelled across with two other young lads from Northern Ireland, Norman Whiteside and Alan Mc Donald, for trials with Manchester United at Old Trafford. Although Colin wasn't taken on there, the Boy's Club leaders didn't give up. They knew he was good. Really good. He was going to make it. They had no doubt about that. But where?

Further trials were arranged with Arsenal, Derby County and Swindon Town.

It was Bryan Hamilton, who was at that time coach of Swindon Town Football Club, who realised that Colin's obvious footballing skills could prove useful to his club in years to come. So Bryan offered the fifteen-year-old the chance to sign a schoolboy contract.

What Colin considered to be the most exciting day of his life up until that time, was when the Club flew his parents and he over from Northern Ireland and he signed up for a soccer apprenticeship at Swindon Town. Step one in the fulfilment of his childhood dream.

It was quite a momentous experience for his parents also. Bryan Hamilton showered them with good old-fashioned Northern Ireland hospitality, making them extremely welcome at the Club, and then whisking them off on a whistle-stop tour of the beautiful Wiltshire countryside. But as concerned parents they had their reservations. Colin was so very young. Could he cope with living away from home?

Then as Christians they were worried too. If Colin ever broke into the footballing big-time, would he ever be saved? They knew that their son knew that it was possible to 'gain the whole world and lose your own soul'. But would he care about that if fame and fortune came his way?...

They would just pray. And pray. And pray...

Bryan wanted his latest signing to start with Swindon there and then. Immediately. At fifteen. He offered to arrange for him to complete his remaining year of compulsory education in a local school.

Colin declined that offer. He wanted to finish his schooling at Dundonald. And he didn't feel that he wanted to leave home all that soon, anyhow. It all seemed too much, too soon. Then there was no cast-iron guarantee that he would make the grade at Swindon, either. He would have to prove himself there. An extra year's physical, mental and emotional maturity would always be useful in that respect.

So, much to the relief of his anxious parents, he decided to remain at home for another year.

That twelve-month period seemed to pass very quickly, however. Colin's life took on a very busy, but pleasant, pattern. It was out to Church with his parents every Sunday, off to School with his mates nearly every week-day, and away to Swindon to train with his new club every holiday.

Then the big day came.

The day that he had dreamt about since he was about seven years old.

The day he had been looking forward to for the past year.

The day when Colin Bailie ceased to be a schoolboy and set out, alone, to be what he had always wanted to be. A professional footballer.

Yet it didn't prove to be the magic experience that he had imagined it would be. Walking away down that long corridor at Belfast International Airport, trying to be brave about it, having just turned his back on his loving Christian parents, who were also trying valiantly to be brave about it, was the most difficult thing that he had ever done so far.

Colin went to live in a player's hostel supervised by Mr. and Mrs. Rideout. They understood football, and footballers, for their son Paul was involved in the game, becoming a very successful player himself. There were six lads in a bedroom in that hostel. Most of the other lads could go home for a short spell every so often, when not playing or training, but because of the distance and expense involved, Colin only made it home twice each year during the playing season.

Yet every time he was back at home he attended Sandown Free Presbyterian Church with the family. Not that he was at all interested in the Gospel or the things of God, but he had a tremendous respect for his parents, and their beliefs. So he went along every weekend that he was at home. Unquestioningly.

Although he was removed from the caring and godly influence of his parents, when over in Swindon, there were those who saw his need of company and friendship. And were very kind to him. Bryan Hamilton invited Colin along to his local Methodist Church once. Colin went, out of a sense of respect for the coach, but there was nothing in the service that touched him in any way.

There was one member of the Swindon Town first-team squad who took a special, deep and prayerful interest in the talented young lad from Northern Ireland. He was Jim Allan. The goalkeeper. After coming to know Colin, and hearing snippets from his background, Jim realised that Colin's Christian parents back at home would be concerned, not only for his physical, but also his spiritual welfare. Jim was a dedicated Christian from Inverness, Scotland. Knowing what it was like to be a young man away from home, he decided to do what he could to help, wherever and whenever possible.

Jim also invited Colin along to the church which he attended, one Sunday. Colin went. For he held that goal-keeper in high regard. He was a player who lived his faith, both on and off the pitch.

At Jim's church, Colin heard the Gospel. Just like at home. But it just washed over him. He had no time for such things. All he wanted to do was perform well in training. Then become a regular member of the first team panel.

That was all that mattered to him at that time. That was why he had left home in the first place. That was why he had endured all the lonely nights and homesick days. And that was what he had set his sights upon. It was his goal. His target. His next objective...

Jim Allan knew that Colin wasn't only a footballer. He loved sport of all kinds. So he invited the promising young sportsman along to some of the meetings arranged by an organisation called Christians in Sport. There he heard the testimonies of people like Joe Brown, the chief scout from Manchester United, and Gerald Williams, the tennis commentator.

Very intriguing, they were. Very impressive, even.

But he was determined that salvation wasn't for him. In the meantime, at least. Being saved never cost him a thought. His mind had been hi-jacked by Satan, and was being driven off at speed in the direction of his unfolding dreams...

It only took six months for Colin to achieve another of his ambitions. By the end of the 1982-83 season he had become established as the regular left full back for Swindon Town Football Club, who were then playing in the old Fourth Division.

For the next two years Colin's football improved and he enjoyed playing in the matches every Saturday, and occasionally during the week. But he was still very homesick. There were long, bleak winter weeks when he yearned for the company, comforts and care of the home he had left behind in Dundonald.

After playing over one hundred and thirty first-team games for Swindon, Colin transferred to Reading at the commencement of the 1985-86 season. That was a move up for the ambitious young player as his new club were in the Third Division. Then things improved again. At the end of that season they were promoted again. Into the Second Division.

Things were on the up and up!

Colin's footballing prospects were looking brighter by the month. He was now playing well in a successful team. Since his talent was now beginning to be appreciated, he also began to see another of those far off childhood dreams realised. He was starting to make money. Real money. For the first time in his life. Bonuses were big. And regular. In the Second Division, too, he had begun to play his football at some of the well-known grounds. Like Elland Road, Leeds, Maine Road, Manchester, and Ewood Park, Blackburn.

It was in May, 1988, that Colin Bailie saw his most fantastic dream come true. He had become a professional footballer. 'Across the water'. That was good. He had started to make money. That was great. And very useful.

Now, his club, Reading, had won through to meet Luton Town in the final of the Simod Cup. At Wembley Stadium!

What an unbelievable thrill it was for the young man from Dundonald to run out, with his teammates, on to the famous turf, to the deafening roar of a sixty-two thousand crowd! The whole atmosphere was awesome. The stadium was a bubbling cauldron of noise and excitement.

Then after ninety minutes hectic play, the crowning glory of crowning glories... Colin's team won! Reading United beat Luton Town by four goals to one. So Colin Bailie came away from Wembley Stadium with a cup-winner's medal!

He had made it in football.

But had he made it in life?

His parents and concerned Christian friends didn't altogether think so. They were praying earnestly for something else. Something different. Something vastly more important..

Sometimes, in football, as in life, the heady glory days are followed in quick succession by a series of hit-you-a-kick-in-the-teeth, down-to-earth-with-a-bump days.

That happened to Colin's club, Reading, at the end of that season, for although they had won the Simod Cup they came bottom of their Division, and were relegated. Back down into the Third.

The summer of 1988 proved to be an unforgettable one for Colin, for a number of reasons. Significant events began to occur. All on the top of one other. And by far the most thrilling of these was that he and Mandy were married.

During his years with Swindon Town, Colin had met Mandy at a Speedway testimonial for a famous rider called Phil Crump. They liked each other and started to see each other more and more often.

Then they liked each other even more, and started to call it 'love'. And after five years spent 'going-together' they decided that they wanted to spend the rest of their lives together. They would marry.

When Colin brought his bride-to-be over to Northern Ireland, to meet his family before the wedding, Mandy had a new experience. She heard the Gospel. Although she had been brought up in a loving, caring home, she had never before heard the good news of salvation. Then she went out with her boy-friend, and his parents, to their home church one Sunday, and heard, for the very first time, about the depths of the love of God, and the purpose of the death of Christ. And her need to be saved.

Since they both wanted to be married in a church, Colin and Mandy started to attend an Anglican Church in Swindon. It was not that they were at all keen to attend 'boring' church services. But they needed their name on the member's roll. For the wedding.

The happy young couple entered into the 'holy estate of matrimony' in July, 1988. And as though that weren't a big enough change for both of them to cope with, they moved more than one hundred miles away to set up their new home. In East Anglia. For during the 'close season' Colin had transferred to Cambridge United, and was due to commence playing for his new club in August.

The next three years were spent chasing fame and fortune in football. Colin was promoted to team captain at Cambridge, and led his team back to Wembley. To the Fourth Division play-offs. Which they won. They were then in the Third Division. Which they won at the end of the next season. So Cambridge United, captained by Colin Bailie, were due to commence the 1991-92 season playing in the Second Division. Up with the big boys again.

Colin had wonderful plans. If they win that Division next year, just look where they would be. Up with the big-big big boys...

It was then that God stepped into Colin's life. To reveal His plans. And answer the prayers of a family and their friends for more than twenty years.

On every occasion when Colin and Mandy came over to visit Colin's parents for a weekend, they went out to church. As a matter of habit. It was taken for granted. That was what you did.

One weekend in June, 1991, they had brought their first little daughter, Laura, over to visit her doting grandparents. So they would go to church as usual.

On the Saturday night, Colin suggested something to Mandy. It was another of his long time, but perhaps not just as passionately pursued ambitions. It came farther down his list of Things-to-do-in-my-lifetime. But it was there, nonetheless.

He wanted to hear Dr. Ian Paisley preaching.

For years he had admired 'the big man', as he used to refer to him, when trying to help his English-born wife make some kind of sense of 'the Northern Ireland situation'. But he had seen him, in the flesh, only once. And that was on a plane between Belfast and London. Dr. Paisley had been sitting about ten rows in front of him. Not the best situation for hearing what the man had to say!

When Mandy heard her huband's proposition she was really enthusiastic about it. She appeared excited, even. This pleased Colin. It was all set up. They would hear the fearless politician, as a faithful preacher, in the morning.

As they had arranged, Colin and Mandy set off for church that Sunday morning, 16th June, 1991, themselves. Nanny and Grandad Bailie had willingly volunteered to keep little Laura, and allow them out together.

It was a beautiful morning as they drove down the Ravenhill Road. Warm, with the scent of summer. When they stepped out of the car at Martyrs Memorial Free Presbyterian Church, Colin was very conscious of the sound of the church bells. Ringing out all over the city. This was Belfast.

Colin and Mandy entered the church, not knowing quite what to expect. Did Dr. Paisley preach to a congregation of hundreds? Or would it be packed? Would there be thousands?

As it turned out the Church was almost full. The young couple were shown to a seat, up near the front. And they waited patiently, soaking up the reverent atmosphere. And waiting for the preacher to appear. They were only partly aware of the gentle stir around them as others found a seat.

Then a back door opened and Dr. Paisley emerged.

Colin Bailie had never felt awestruck before, in anybody's presence, and he had met some prominent people in the world of sport. But this man was different. There was something striking about him. Colin felt awestruck now. He gazed up at the platform. Dr. Paisley sat still, with his head bowed. It was obvious that he was engaged in silent prayer. Committing the whole service into the hand of God. Colin had seen this before. Rev. Mc Ilveen did it in Sandown, before a meeting. And so did his parents.

Mandy and her husband exchanged knowing glances. 'So that's him', the glances said. 'There he is. The 'big man'. In person'.

When the man rose and started to speak there began another whole new experience for them. The two first-time visitors to 'The Martyrs' sat mesmerised.

What a strong, commanding, resonant voice!

What a powerful, but somehow peaceful, presence!

Yet again, Colin and Mandy heard the Gospel. Although Dr. Paisley's message, which he had entitled, 'The Effectual Call of the Gospel', had been prepared for Christians, he felt constrained to present the message of life and salvation to his congregation.

Colin was touched by that message. Moved by the Holy Spirit. Convicted.

Having been to many more Free Presbyterian services than his wife, Colin dreaded the end of that meeting coming round. He was sure that the preacher would make some kind of an appeal. And if that happened, what was he going to do?

He wanted to be saved. He knew he must.

But what about his footballing career? Could he have both? Did he really want both? What questions! Brave decisions would have to be made. Sometime.

Towards the end of the service, Dr. Paisley told a story which burned right into Colin's heart and soul. It was about a man who for most of his life-time had held high office. Then he became ill. Gravely, indeed terminally, ill.

When Dr. Paisley heard of his illness, he determined to go and see him. The whole congregation listened intently as the speaker described how he had been driven up a long tree-lined avenue to the sick man's country mansion. It was a magnificent place, dripping with the trappings of wealth and fame.

A butler admitted the visitor and ushered him into the room where the sick man sat. Although obviously very weak, he summoned up enough energy to enquire, with bemused surprise, "What brings you here, Ian?"

"You, and your condition, have brought me here," was the immediate, and earnest reply. With that he began to warn the ill man, with as much tenderness as he could muster, of his need of salvation, and the gravity of his situation.

After a short conversation, both men ended up on their knees, and Dr. Paisley began to pray, aloud, for his sick friend.

Then, all of a sudden, in the middle of the prayer, the man stood up and announced, emphatically, "I don't want to do this!"

Dr. Paisley concluded his story with the remark, "That man had refused God's salvation for the last time. He died a short time later."

Colin felt so sorry for the the man who had died. How crazy! How absolutely stupid of him! Imagine, refusing to be saved, in his condition.

The speaker finished his sermon on a touching note. By way of contrast to his previous story, he told of the funerals of two not-nearly-so-well-off-in-the-world believers, whose funerals he had recently conducted. Their deaths weren't tragedies. They seemed to Colin more like triumphs. Like celebrations. Those people were now, according to Dr. Paisley, "With Christ, in glory."

Colin thought again. "How could anybody be prepared to face death like that?" That seemed crazy, too.

As he sat there, he became lost in his own thoughts. The burning arrows of conviction were piercing deep into his heart one after another. And he seemed to have no defence. He couldn't stop them...

Although he had felt sorry for the sick man who had spurned salvation during his last days on earth, he was doing exactly the same thing! Refusing to come to Christ. And be saved. If he died it certainly wouldn't be a triumph. It would be more like a tragedy...

The service ended and a hymn was sung. There was no prolonged appeal and Colin was glad about that. Mandy and he would just slip out and go home. He determined, though, that he would have to settle this business about salvation. Sometime.

While standing with all the others in the aisle, waiting to leave the church, Colin decided that he would speak to Dr. Paisley on the way out. Just make himself known to 'the big man'.

When Mandy and he stepped forward to speak to him, Dr. Paisley asked, "And where are you pair from?"

"We are from Cambridge. We are over here for the weekend," Colin explained. "We are staying with my parents. I'm sure you know them. My father is Jim Bailie. He sings."

"Oh, of course I know Jim Bailie," was the preacher's reply. And then his next question changed the subject completely.

"And do you know the Saviour?" he enquired, point blank.

Mandy hung her head. Colin whispered, "No."

"Well, do you want to know Him?" was the earnest soul-winner's next question.

Colin became acutely aware of the dozens of people, patiently queued up behind them, waiting to leave. But he had been confronted, fairly and squarely, as never before, with the claims of Christ. He had to do something about it now. And he had to answer the question, too.

After a few seconds hesitation he confessed, quietly, "Yes. I would like to be saved."

An elder conducted the young couple round to a little room at the back of the building, behind the pulpit.

While sitting there Colin emerged from a mental haze to the realization that Mandy was with him. He knew why he had been asked to wait behind here. But did she? He didn't want her to be forced into anything that she wasn't prepared for. Yet he wanted her by his side.

It was a bit awkward.

Turning, with a faint half-smile, he looked right into her eyes, and asked, "Do you know what we are doing in here, Mandy?"

"Yes, I know," she replied, appearing both genuinely composed and quietly confident. "And I'm staying with you."

They lapsed into reflective silence. To wait.

In the silence the Devil stepped up his attack on Colin's reeling mind. "You can't do this," he seemed to be repeating. "You don't even want to do this. Think of your career. And the Second Division..."

That was countered by the voice of the Holy Spirit. Drawing. Calling. Urging. "Stay here. Go in for salvation. Don't miss it..."

The battle for the soul of Colin Bailie was in full swing, when the door opened, and Dr. Paisley came in. It was only about five minutes since they had last seen him at the church door. But Colin felt that this struggle in his soul had been raging for about five hours.

When they were all settled down, Dr. Paisley began to talk to the young couple. Gently, but persuasively. Colin and Mandy had a number of questions to ask. The big preacher, who, despite his many commitments, seemed to have endless time for them, answered every query, softly.

Then, like gentleness itself, Dr. Ian Paisley led Colin and his wife, both, to faith in Christ.

They all knelt down, together. Colin prayed, aloud, first. Clearly. Sincerely. "Please God, would You forgive my sins and let Jesus, Your Son, come into my life," he asked. Then, after a pause, he added, "And please help me to live the Christian life."

Now it was Mandy's turn. She prayed, too. Not having been brought up in an evangelical background, however, she didn't 'speak the language.' So her prayer was refreshingly uncluttered. She simply asked God to save her. And sure as His Word, He did. Instantly.

When all three rose to their feet, a few minutes later, the newly-converted couple prepared to leave. Dr. Paisley gave them some tracts and booklets to read, and some sound advice about the way ahead. Then he left them with the assurance, "Goodbye now. May God richly bless you both. I will be praying for you."

As Colin walked back out to the car he was in tears. Weeping silently. Mandy noticed it, but didn't say anything. She was having bother enough coming to terms with her own emotions.

As they drove back up to the house, both Colin and Mandy were each totally engrossed with their own thoughts and feelings. They were deeply moved. Dazed. Numb, almost. So neither spoke. For neither was sure just exactly what to say to be right.

When they arrived at the Bailie home, though, everything changed. In one happy, blissful moment. By way of explaining the marvellously mixed-up state of both Mandy and himself, Colin exclaimed, when he had both parents together, "We have just got saved!"

The faces of Jim and Helen Bailie were an absolute picture. Their expressions showed a delighted surprise that verged on incredulity. They could just hardly believe it!

All those prayers of all those years had been answered. And two of them at once! It was fantastic! They all hugged each other. Everybody seemed to be smiling and weeping all at the same time!

The joy that Colin's parents had expressed so spontaneously was infectious by nature. It was soon transmitted to their newly-born-again son and his newly-born-again wife. Through their reaction Colin and Mandy began to realize the long-term significance of each of their individual decisions on that wonderful morning. They were now children of God through their faith in Christ Jesus. Safe for time and eternity. God was their Father. And heaven was their home.

It was nearly incomprehensible!

An hour or two later they were to learn something else as well. Their coming to the Saviour was important not only to God, themselves, and their immediate family, but it mattered to other Christians, too. They were now one in Christ with all other true believers.

After the initial euphoria had subsided a bit, Colin's dad remarked, "Tommy Jordan has prayed for this moment ever since you left home, Colin. Every week at the Friday night prayer meeting, without fail, he asked God to preserve you and save you."

Colin was touched.

He loved the Jordans. They were both good and godly people. And Tommy had been praying for him for years, also. Marvellous!

When they returned to England, rejoicing in their newly-found faith, Colin had soon to go back into serious training with Cambridge United. The new season began in August.

There was a totally different emphasis in his life then, though. As soon as he arrived home after that weekend when he and Mandy were saved, Colin unearthed the still-brand-new-looking Bible which Rev. David Mc Ilveen had given to the newly-weds three years previously. And he started to read it. He started to devour it. In every spare minute he had for the next two or three weeks Colin read that Bible.

That was when he began to appreciate the efforts of John Brown and the other teachers in Brooklands Gospel Hall Sunday School. They had encouraged him to learn a number of Scripture passages. And now they came back to him. He knew where they were in his Bible. So he returned to them often.

His favourite passage for many weeks was one that John Brown had taught him, back in those early childhood days. It was John 14 vs 1-6. In it, Jesus spoke to his disciples about 'many mansions'. The word 'mansions' transported Colin right back to the June morning when Dr. Paisley's story, about the man in the mansion who had rejected God's salvation, made such a profound impression on him.

What a contrast! Now there were 'many masions' prepared for Mandy and himself!

Colin also wanted to worship God. And go to church on a regular basis. To meet other Christians. So for a few Sundays he attended the little Baptist Hall in the village where they lived. Numbers were very small, but the Pastor was very faithful in his presentation of the Word of God. From the biggest Bible that Colin had ever seen!

The Christians there would have loved to have the young couple join them in their fellowship, but Colin and Mandy had already arranged to move into the city of Cambridge to be nearer Colin's work. So they soon moved on.

When the new season began, Colin was in a dilemma. He had a problem. He knew that he ought to come out boldly and witness to his faith. But he was scared. Although he had never been afraid of any player, either on or off the pitch, Colin didn't have the courage to witness to his teammates about his faith. So he consoled himself with a compromise. He would live it. Not preach it.

It wasn't long until he had a pattern worked out for himself. After 'home' matches he declined to go out and socialise with the others, as once he did. Instead he went home to Mandy and little Laura. When the team stayed overnight in a hotel at 'away' matches, the players usually 'roomed' in pairs. So Colin prayed and read the Gideon Bible in the bedroom before retiring for the night.

He soon discovered, though, that although he loved actually playing the game, his taste buds for the whole footballing scenario had gone. He determined that he would quit the game at the end of the season. Even if Cambridge were promoted into the new Premier League that was being planned.

As the year progressed, however, some things started happening at the club which Colin wasn't happy about. One of these, against which he protested very strongly, was the manner in which some of the younger players were being treated. When his repeated objections, as club captain, were ignored, he resigned. Before his end-of-the-season deadline.

Having left Cambridge United, Colin had no job. Now though, he had Someone to whom he could turn in times of difficulty and trial. His all-loving, all-caring all-powerful Heavenly Father. So he prayed. And Mandy prayed.

When Colin had a telephone call from Martin O'Neill they wondered if this was the answer to their prayers. Martin had heard of Colin's resignation from Cambridge and he was just wondering if he would be willing to play a few games for his club, Wycombe Wanderers.

Colin decided to give it a try.

He played a few matches for Wycombe. Something more important than playing a few games of football took place in Colin's life during his short stay at the non-league club, though. It was there that God endued him with the courage to witness to his faith in Christ to his new boss. Martin had a few caustic comments to make about 'religion in Northern Ireland' and a few quaint quips to crack about Dr. Paisley. Although Martin didn't appear interested in what he had to say, the actual experience of speaking to someone about the Lord was a big breakthrough for Colin, who came to realize something else in those few weeks, as well. It was that although a number of Christian players, whom he highly respected, continued both to play well and witness effectively in the game, football, in future, was not for him.

So he took a bold step of faith. He left the game. Quit, completely.

Now he had a real problem. He had no other job. And the only thing which he had ever done, since he was fifteen years of age, was play football.

He applied for training in the police. And waited. Whilst his application was being processed, Mandy went out to work. To help pay the bills.

For eight trying months, Colin and Mandy prayed and relied on their God who had saved them and given them so much. It was hard, though, sometimes.

Then came the answer to their prayers. Colin was accepted as a police recruit, in February, 1993. Since then he and his family have moved to the north of England where he now serves as an officer in the force.

As they look back on their lives, Colin and Mandy have much for which they thank God.

They praise Him for the little family with which He has blessed them. Their two much-loved daughters, Laura and Lucy. And Colin's job which he enjoys.

Then there are Colin's parents, Sunday School teachers in Brooklands Gospel Hall and Christians from Sandown Free Presbyterian Church who prayed for them before they came to know the Lord.

And Dr. Ian Paisley who so gently and tenderly pointed them to the Saviour.

But above and beyond all, they thank Him for ever saving them, and giving them a whole new direction in life. They are now playing in the REAL Premier League. The one that matters. Paul described it as pressing 'toward the mark for the prize of the high calling of God in Christ Jesus'. (Phil. 3 v.14)

A different set of goalposts!

24

STAND BACK AND WATCH
GOD AT WORK

❖

Conditions in the only hotel in Ebolowa, Cameroon, West
Africa, could only be described as basic. Extremely basic.
'Facilities' were non-existent. And it was in that hotel,
La Ranche, which had once been classified as 'the worst hotel in
Africa', that Dr. Ian Paisley and Rev. David Mc Ilveen began the day
on Sunday, 11th January, 1998.

They met for prayer in Dr. Paisley's room, asking God for His
guidance throughout the day.

At ten o'clock in the morning, with the thermometer rising steadily, they met with a group of church elders and at eleven they went
into the main building of the Orthodox Presbyterian Church in
Ebolowa, for the morning service.

What a sight met their gaze as they emerged from the room at the
back! There were people sitting everywhere! One thousand six
hundred men, women and children were packed into and onto any
and every available space. And there were nearly two hundred more

who hadn't managed to gain admission at all. They were standing around outside, straining to gaze in through the open windows!

When the service began with prayer and praise, the visitors were held spellbound by the singing, particularly. Several choirs from the church took part. There were youth choirs and adult choirs. Their singing was enthusiastic but respectful. The harmony was beautiful.

The atmosphere was reverent, but expectant...

When Dr. Paisley rose to speak, an awesome hush settled upon the congregation. After he had read from the Scriptures, the speaker whom they had all been waiting to hear, sounded out the Gospel message very clearly, through an interpreter. No one was left in any doubt as to why Christ Jesus had come into the world. It was 'to save sinners.'

As the meeting progressed, the silent stillness began to be punctuated by the sounds of sobbing. The piercing point of the sword of the Spirit, the Word of God, was beginning to penetrate hearts. Convict souls.

At the close of the service, Dr. Paisley made an appeal, urging those who were still unsaved, to respond to the Gospel invitation. And come to the Saviour. And in that large church, with its capacity crowd and Spirit-filled atmosphere, seventy people moved forward slowly to the front to be counselled by the local pastors.

Before everyone left for home, and nobody really seemed to want to do that anyway, all those who had been saved at that service assembled at the front of the building. To have a group photograph taken with Dr. Paisley.

This was to prove more than just a collective record of a very special movement of God. It was, for each of those newly-saved individuals, a very practical testimony of their conversion. They were demonstrating to their friends and relatives, many of whom would be bitterly opposed to the Gospel, that they were now identified with Christ, and His Church.

Over lunch in the pastor's house there was much rejoicing at what God had done that morning. The word 'revival' was on a number of lips. And the day was by no means over yet. There was more to come...

Around two o'clock in the afternoon, Dr. Paisley and Rev. Mc Ilveen, who was the 'official driver' for the tour, left Ebolowa in a four-track vehicle. They were on their way, as they thought, to another church, up the country.

For the first mile or so, the journey was fine. On a half-decent road. Then things became more difficult. The road, as such, disappeared. Became little more than a mud track. Still they kept going. But only for a while.

Five miles out from Ebolowa they came upon an obstacle on the road. One which proved impossible to either get around, or over. A large digger had partially left the road, blocking their route completely.

They had no option but to turn back and proceed to another church, whose members were expecting a visit from Dr. Paisley at some time during that day.

When they arrived at that particular church, more than twenty miles north-west of Ebolowa, it was late afternoon. Around five o'clock. They discovered a large and eager crowd awaiting them there, however. They hadn't given up hope of hearing Dr. Paisley. And they had been there from nine o'clock in the morning!

Two factors prompted the long-awaited speaker to ask that the service be held in the open-air, if possible.

The first was the heat. By that time the temperature had climbed to 36 degrees C, and the two travelling ministers, who had recently arrived in from a Northern Ireland January, were sweltered!

And the second, very practical reason, was the crowd. There was no way whatsoever that the little church at Mindiml was going to hold the four hundred or so people who had gathered for the service.

This permission was readily granted, with everybody agreeing that it was a very sensible idea.

When a few rearrangements had been made, Dr. Paisley preached the Gospel once more, standing in the shade below the eaves of the church building.

And again souls were moved by the message.

When an appeal was made, at the close of that meeting, for those who were anxious to know their sins forgiven, and Christ as their

Saviour, to come forward for counselling, more than forty people responded. Walking out in the open-air, late on into an African evening. Wanting to be saved.

Those people, of all ages, were spoken to, and led to the Lord, by local pastors and Christian leaders.

It was approaching midnight when Dr. Paisley and his travelling companion eventually returned to their Ebolowa no-star hotel.

They were tired, thirsty, and thrilled.

Jaded but joyful.

Fatigued but fulfilled.

They met for praise in Dr. Paisley's room, thanking God for His guidance throughout the day.

Reporting home by telephone, telling all the praying friends back in Northern Ireland about that memorable Sunday, Dr. Paisley said, "We were just compelled to stand back and watch God at work."

That wasn't a new experience for him, however.

He has been doing it now for over fifty years.

25

LITTLE LOST SHEEP

❖

The crowd of children packed into the upstairs room of Hill Street Baptist Church, in Ballymena, sat transfixed. The pastor's wife, who had started a meeting once a week for the boys and girls of the town, held her audience enthralled.

She was a marvellous storyteller.

And she had a marvellous story to tell.

It was the story of the Gospel.

The lady had read to them from Luke chapter 15 in her Bible. About a lost sheep. And she was now in the process of explaining the story to them. She painted the picture of the 'little lost sheep' in such graphic detail and with such genuine sincerity, that there was an air of eagerness, of expectancy, about the gathering.

Discipline wasn't a problem. Children were hanging on her every word. There was a real sense of the presence of God in that room.

"Just think about that poor little sheep," she challenged her captivated child congregation. "Out on the mountains. Lost. Alone. Hungry. Exhausted. What could happen to it?"

There then followed a deliberate silence to allow the young minds to imagine their worst possible outcome, before she elaborated ...

"Well, it could easily fall foul of the elements. Up there in the hills it gets so cold at night. It could freeze to death in a very short space of time, if it didn't have any protection ...

And it was an easy prey for the wild animals, too. It was so weak. What would happen if a lion, or a bear, or some other hungry animal came along? What hope was there for it? What chance would it have? It couldn't put up much of a fight, could it? ...

Then what about somebody wanting to steal it? In those days there were many thieves about. A tired, lost sheep would be easy to bundle up and take home. To sell. Or keep. It would never see its friends in its flock again ...

And worst of all, it could be killed."

A hushed horror hung over the hall.

"You see," the leader continued, in subdued tones, "many people in those days were greedy for money. So they would think nothing of killing a poor lost sheep. And selling it for meat to hungry people. Or indeed, desperate, hungry people might just kill it. To eat themselves ..."

Another purposeful pause. To allow the grim prospects for a little lost sheep to tumble around in stirred imaginations.

Then came the turning point of the narrative.

"Was there any hope at all for this poor sheep?" the speaker prodded.

"Remember, it couldn't do anything for itself. It was lost. Had no idea where it was. So it couldn't find its way home. And anyway, even if it did know the way home, it was so tired, so weak, so exhausted, so helpless, it was in no fit state to go anywhere. It just wanted to lie down, and sleep, and sleep, and it would probably ..."

Having painted the blackest, bleakest picture that words could conjure up, the pastor's wife pulled open the curtains of hope. Ever so slightly. To let in just a cheerful chink of light. To brighten the gloom.

"Yes, thankfully, there was hope for it. Not in itself. But with the shepherd. When he discovered that it was missing, he would set out to search for it. To find it. No matter what the cost. He wouldn't just say to himself, 'Sure I have a whole foldfull of sheep here. I will just let that one go. It was always a bit of a nuisance anyway.' No. He would go out after it. And it would be very hard and dangerous for him, too ..."

Then, suddenly, to emphasise her point, she interrupted the narrative.

"A man once wrote a hymn about this," she explained, "and I am going to sing some of it to you."

And without further ado, she began to sing, in her strong, tuneful voice:-

'There were ninety and nine that safely lay
In the shelter of the fold,
But one was out on the hills away,
Far off from the gates of gold,
Away on the mountains wild and bare,
Away from the tender Shepherd's care.

"Lord, Thou hast here Thy ninety and nine,
Are they not enough for Thee?"
But the Shepherd made answer, "This of Mine
Has wandered away from Me;
And although the road be rough and steep,
I go to the desert to find My sheep." ...

And all through the mountains thunder-riven,
And up from the rocky steep,
There arose a glad cry to the gate of heaven
"Rejoice! I have found my sheep!"
And the angels echoed around the throne,
"Rejoice! for the Lord brings back His own!"'

The children were filled with a sense of admiring awe as their leader sang. It was nothing new to them to hear her burst out into song. She did it often. But they never failed to be impressed with the fact that she always sang the same way as she spoke. With absolute conviction.

When the strains of 'the ninety-and-nine' had died away, the pastor's wife went on where she left off. She was now ready to apply the story. Challenge her young listeners with the truth of the gospel. That was her sole aim in life. To see people led to the Saviour.

"Do you know who the little lost sheep is, in the story, boys and girls?" she began. "It tells us about people. All kinds of people. Adults and children alike. The Bible says that we are all sinners and are far away from God. And we are like the poor little sheep, too. Lost, helpless and hopeless. We can do nothing to help ourselves. But the good news is that there is a Shepherd. One who has gone out to look for us. And bring us back safely to His fold."

With that she opened her Bible again, and read John 10 v 11. "I am the good shepherd: the good shepherd giveth his life for the sheep."

Closing her Bible over, with a finger still in the place, the pastor's wife continued, "We all know who said that, don't we? Yes, of course. It was the Lord Jesus. He is the Good Shepherd ..." And from there she proceeded to explain how that Lord Jesus had come into the world to 'seek and to save the lost'. And to 'give his own life for the sheep'.

The Gospel message was so tenderly, and yet so clearly and plainly presented that not one single child in that attentive audience could miss but understand what it was all about.

When most of the other children had gone out to go home, and the pastor's wife was tidying up to go home herself, a little boy who had been hanging around, with a heavy heart, slipped up to her side.

It was her six-year-old son.

"Mummy," he said, with his heartache trembling in his voice, "I don't want to be a lost sheep. I want to be a saved lamb."

His mother was wise. She knew instinctively that 'the Lord had called the child'. And she was delighted. After all, she had been praying that God would save this boy since away long before he was born.

"That's good, son," she replied, gently, "We will go downstairs into the main church where it is quiet, and talk to God about it."

When mother and son had gone down into the silent and almost sacred, echoey emptiness of the main church, they knelt down, side by side, at the second pew from the back.

And there, that lady who had presented the Gospel message with such vivid clarity to a roomful of children, presented that same message with the same earnestness and genuine enthusiasm to one single child. Her own son.

As they knelt there, mother beside her boy, the little lad simply trusted in Jesus Christ as his Saviour. And in one sincere act of child-like faith he changed flocks. The lost sheep had become, as God, his parents and himself, had desired, a saved lamb.

Not only was he now the son of a Baptist pastor and his wife. He was the child of a King. An heir of God and a joint-heir with Jesus Christ. But he didn't know anything about any of that at the time. For he was still only six!

It was 29th May, 1932, an early summer evening, and still clear, as they left the church for their home next door. As he looked around the church and passed through the garden which divided it from the manse, that little boy seemed to see things in a different light. A tremendous sense of joy and peace and at-oneness with God flooded into, through and over his soul.

He was happy. Content. Satisfied.

He was saved.

That young lad developed quickly. Both spiritually and physically. He loved his Lord. He loved his Bible. And he also loved going to meetings where he heard his father, and occasionally his mother, expound the Word of God, and preach the Gospel.

He also loved the country, and the uncluttered, uncomplicated country way of life. So he decided, in his early teenage, that he would like to be a farmer, when he eventually stopped, 'growing up'.

That was it. All worked out in his mind. He would go to Green-mount Agricultural College when he left School. Then get a job on a farm. Maybe, then, after that, who knows, he might even buy his own farm ...

Dreaming was free.

But he had to start somewhere.

So on Saturdays he went out to work on the farms of some friends, outside Ballymena, and in the school holidays he started to stay away on farms farther afield. All to gain experience. It would be good to know what he was talking about when he went for his interview at Greenmount! When he was just fifteen years of age, this young man went to stay with George Watson and his family, near Sixmilecross, in Co. Tyrone. It was during the Easter holidays. And it was great.

There was nothing to beat the freedom of the country. He used to love to guide the team of two horses as they patiently plodded, pulling the plough, up and down, up and down the field. It was a challenge to keep the furrow straight, but the young man was rapidly developing strong arms and a strong voice, so he managed to keep the team in order. The smell of the damp-but-drying upturned earth, the wheeling birds ready to snatch a tasty meal, and the warmth of the spring sun on his back, were just wonderful. If he hadn't been well taught that heaven was still up ahead, he would have thought that this was it!

George Watson was more than merely an ordinary hard-working Co. Tyrone farmer, however. He was an earnest Christian with a burning desire to see others saved. And he realised that this strapping part-time farmboy of his needed to learn more than just how to plough fields, milk cows, and cut turf. He needed to learn how to preach the Gospel.

There was no doubt whatsoever in the farmer's mind that this teenager had all the qualifications required. He had the faith, the desire and the background. All he needed was the chance.

And he was in a position to give him that.

One day he said to the young would-be-farmer, "You should try and give us a wee word some Sunday down in the Hall. We would all love to hear you."

The youth was pleased to be asked, and agreed to give it a try.

So a date was arranged.

Then the preparation began. He thought, and prayed. And wrote notes and scribbled them out again. Then he thought more. And prayed more. And eventually prepared his sermon. It would be good. He knew that.

When the big Sunday came, the audience at Sixmilecross Evangelistic Hall was far from big. There was George Watson, his wife, and their son. There was Bob Kyle, and his two boys. And another woman whom the preacher-for-the-day didn't know.

Seven of them altogether.

After all the prayer, and all the preparation, when the teenage speaker stood up to present this powerful message about 'The Man Who Fell Among Thieves", he suffered the same fate himself. He fell among thieves. Three of them.

One ran off with his confidence, and he began to tremble like a leaf in an autumn breeze. So much so that he had to hold on tightly to the platform for support.

The second thief stole his mobility, so that he couldn't move. Not one single bit of him. Not even his tongue. It felt like a tennis ball in his mouth. A tennis ball that seemed to grow all the time and slow up as it grew bigger. Until it stopped altogether. It just blocked up his mouth. But refused to budge.

The cruellest of all the thieves, though, was the one that robbed him of his memory. Caused him to forget all that he had intended to say. All the 'great points' that he had preached over and over in his mind whilst walking up and down and round and round the farmyard had all disappeared. Evaporated. Into thin air. He couldn't remember another single one of them.

So he did the only thing that he could think of doing in the circumstances.

He sat down. In complete embarrassment and utter confusion.

Before arriving at the hall he had reckoned that this message would take a good twenty minutes to put across. Maybe even half-an-hour.

It had taken exactly four minutes!

George Watson took over, and finished the meeting, but the young man, who had so much relished the opportunity to preach his first sermon, dreaded what he would say to him afterwards. He had been such a complete and absolute flop!

As he was hurriedly gathering together all his belongings to beat a hasty retreat, the older, and much more mature Christian went across to the mortified youth.

There was no sign of a rebuke in his approach. No ridicule. No indication of anger or frustration. His aim was simply to encourage the young fellow whom he knew had spent so many hours in preparation.

"Don't worry, son," he consoled, reassuringly, "if you can preach for four minutes when you are fifteen, when you are seventy you will probably be able to preach for a week!"

That, at least, was comforting. And George Watson gave the young lad yet another chance to prove himself as a preacher. During the summer time. When his willing farmhand came over to stay and help bring home the turf, he preached on another Sunday. And this time things went better. The Gospel message was clearly proclaimed. All the 'thieves' who had robbed the aspiring preacher of his confidence, his speech, his points and ultimately his pride, on the previous occasion, had been captured and put into prison somewhere. And they were handcuffed hand and foot too, by the prayers of well-wishing Christian friends.

His experiences in the heart of County Tyrone did two things for that young man. The first was that they left him with a deep feeling for the Evangelistic Hall at Sixmilecross. He felt that it was an essential part of his being. An old friend. So intense was this affinity with that unimposing building in which he made his first venture into preaching, that he made his first venture into poetry, writing about it.

The poem is simple, but powerful. It will probably never make it into 'Palgrave's Golden Treasury' or 'The Nation's Hundred Favourite Poems', but it served the purpose of the poet.

It expressed his feelings about that old Hall precisely. At fifteen, coming sixteen.

The Evangelistic Hall, Sixmilecross

Just down the road from Sixmilecross,
On the road to Carrickmore,
There in a field beside that road,
There stands a little hall.

It is not a stately building,
With pillars straight and tall,
It is a little building,
Where sinners hear the call.

Every Sunday at four o'clock
Some saved ones here do meet,
And sinners, too, do hear the Word,
Of which they truly need.

Here some good Gospel hymns are sung,
And prayers are faithfully given,
To Him who saved us by His Word,
And made us fit for heaven.

No modernisitc doctrines taught,
No 'Isms' of the day,
We stand for nothing but the Book,
The good old Gospel way.

It is what Calvin stood for,
John Knox, he preached it too,
For it the Covenanters died,
And we believe it's true.

The second effect that the Sixmilecross experience had on the mid-teenager was that it changed his whole ambition in life. With a developing zeal for God and an acquired taste for preaching, he realised that he wanted to spend his life as a preacher. Not as a farmer.

He wanted to see souls saved. Not bodies fed.

He longed to provide spiritual, not physical, food.

So, believing it to be God's will for his life, that young man enrolled in the Barry School of Evangelism in Wales, and after a year's study there, completed three more years at the Theological Hall of the Reformed Presbyterian Church in Ireland.

He was training to be a minister of the Gospel.

On 1st August, 1946, when twenty years of age, that young preacher was ordained as minister of Ravenhill Evangelical Mission Church. Rev. W. J. Grier, BA, Evangelical Presbyterian, preached the ordination sermon, Prof. T. B. McFarlane, BA, Reformed Presbyterian offered prayer and Rev. Thomas Rowan, MA, Irish Presbyterian, gave the charge to the congregation.

At the service, his father, Rev. J. Kyle Paisley gave the ordination charge to his son, taking as his theme some of the last recorded words of Paul. His charge to another evolving servant of God, his understudy, Timothy. He urged his son to, 'Preach the word; be instant, in season, out of season; reprove, rebuke, exhort with all longsuffering and doctrine ... endure afflictions, do the work of an evangelist, make full proof of thy ministry.' (2 Tim. 4 vs 1-5.) He quoted the following lines from the hymn 'The Mighty Ordination':

From the glory and the gladness
From His secret place,
From the rapture of His presence,
From His radiant face.
Christ the Son of God hath sent me,
Through the midnight lands,
Mine the mighty ordination
Of the piercéd hands

That was a memorable service. The beginning of a lifetime of challenge. And one of the biggest challenges of that lifetime of ministry came the very next Sunday morning ...

It often makes young and relatively inexperienced preachers nervous when they discover older and more experienced preachers in their audiences. But when this newly-ordained minister realised that the renowned Rev W.P. Nicholson was sitting in the back seat, to hear him deliver his first message, as a minister of that church, he was terrified. Scared stiff. Absolutely petrified. For, in addition to being a dynamic preacher, whom God had used mightily, this W.P. Nicholson, was not one, apparently, who was noted for his tact and diplomacy. He had a habit of saying exactly what he thought!

However, the twenty year old minister began to preach. He had to! He had no other choice! Since it was to be his first sermon in charge of that church, he had resolved to let everybody know what he stood for. And what he was there for. He was 'setting out his stall'. His text was, 'For I determined not to know anything among you, save Jesus Christ, and him crucified.' (1 Cor. 2v2)

The new preacher, in his new pulpit, preached with all his heart. Gave it 'his best shot'. An evident sense of the presence and power of God permeated the place.

Just after he had finished speaking, Mr Nicholson came forward to the front of the church, rapped the Communion Table sharply with his knuckles, and asked, gruffly, "Young man, have you ever seen a cow's tongue?"

Belfast's Ravenhill Road seemed a million miles removed from the depths of County Tyrone, but that puzzled preacher's mind flashed back to the little byre in Sixmilecross. The singular smell, the peculiar steamy warmth, the big tongues curling round and swirling up the hay before them.

"Yes, sir," he answered, in all truth.

"Well, tell me then, what is it like?" the famous preacher persisted.

The man in the pulpit wondered what all this was leading to, but he replied, "It is like a file."

Then William P. Nicholson lifted a hand to heaven, closed his eyes, and offered an unusual 'prayer of dedication' for the minister who was embarking upon a lifetime of service for God.

"Lord, give this young man a tongue like an old cow," he entreated.

That minister has now preached faithfully for over fifty years, since those early, fiery days of first sermons.

In that time he has been privileged to see God's rich blessing upon his ministry. Thousands of souls have been saved. And he has witnessed over one hundred churches established around the world. Although many of these are in Northern Ireland, there are others in various locations across the British Isles, U.S.A., Canada, Australia, and Jamaica. And there is a flourishing and fruitful missionary work in both Africa and South America.

And the young man's name?

Well, you've guessed it, haven't you?

The little lost sheep who became a little saved lamb ...

Ian Paisley.

OTHER BOOKS BY THE SAME AUTHOR:

MY FATHER'S HAND

THIS IS FOR REAL

JUST THE WAY I AM

SOME PARTY IN HEAVEN

FIRST CITIZEN SMYTH

SOMETHING WORTH LIVING FOR

HOW SWEET THE SOUND